WHAS Crusade for Children · 1954-2001
48

1997
44 YEARS
WHAS Crusade for Children

WHAS CRUSADE for CHILDREN
35 YEARS OF CARING
1954-1988

II

WHAS CRUSADE FOR CHILDREN
29

32
CRUSADE FOR CHILDREN
WHAS

20

14

21
WHAS CRUSADE FOR CHILDREN

WHAS CRUSADE for CHILDREN
45
1954-1998

WHAS CRUSADER FOR CHILDREN 1964

18

WHAS
Twenty-Fourth Crusade for Children

8

WHAS Crusade for Children
30
1954 1983

WHAS CRUSADE FOR CHILDREN
26

16

13

15

23

MIRACLES BY THE MILLION:
50 YEARS OF THE
WHAS CRUSADE FOR CHILDREN

Phyllis Knight

Written By: Bob Hill & Edited By: C. Ray Hall

Book Design: Julius Friedman
and Alexandra Howell

Special thanks to:

Katina Whitlock – archive research and photo research

John Blim and Dan Miller – copy editing

The photographs in this book come from the WHAS Crusade for

Children archives. Many photographers

over the years have contributed their time and talent to take these

photos. Special thanks to The Courier-Journal and Louisville Times

photographers who took many of

the photos from early years of the Crusade when

both WHAS and The Courier-Journal were part

of the Bingham Companies.

This book is made possible by a generous grant from Norton Healthcare

Kosair Children's Hospital
Norton Audubon Hospital
Norton Hospital
Norton Southwest Hospital
Norton Suburban Hospital
Carroll County Hospital
Norton Immediate Care Centers

With gratitude for the community's generosity to

Kosair Children's Hospital and our Norton

hospitals over the past 50 years.

ISBN 0-615-12500-X

CONTENTS

FOREWORD

Fifty years. More than one hundred million dollars. Millions of special needs children helped by agencies funded by the WHAS Crusade for Children.

It is firefighters shaking buckets. The Archdiocese of Louisville parishioners, Norton Healthcare employees, the employees and customers of Kroger and Dairy Queen and many more organizations giving their all. Volunteers, celebrities and WHAS employees giving millions of volunteer hours.

It appears just that simple. But, with closer examination, the WHAS Crusade for Children is bigger than the sum of those parts. It is a cultural phenomenon that crosses all socio-economic, racial, religious and political perspectives to bring everyone together toward a common goal. The Crusade is testimony to the good in people. The Crusade is the best of each one of us – and much bigger than all of us together.

While this book chronicles the past fifty years, it is really a benchmark for the next fifty. The needs among our children will not diminish. With many challenges ahead, we must continue to pull together to ensure the future of the WHAS Crusade for Children. 2003 marks the birth of the WHAS Crusade Endowment. The Endowment, combined with the Crusade's rich history of community support, can ensure the life and growth of the WHAS Crusade for Children.

This book sheds light on our passionate past and promising future. It is both a tribute and a thank you to the pioneers who went before us. It is also a thank you to the thousands of firefighters, volunteers and WHAS employees who work roadblocks, make bologna sandwiches, answer telephones and do so much more. Sincere thanks also go to past and present Crusade board members, advisory board ministers and the new endowment board members. Their diligence and discipline are forging a path to the future.

Please enjoy this labor of love knowing there are limitless opportunities to labor and love in the future. A special thank you to Norton Healthcare as the sponsor of the initial printing, to the artful passion and hard work of Bob Hill, Julius Friedman, and C. Ray Hall, as well as the entire WHAS Crusade for Children staff. Thank you all for supporting the WHAS Crusade for Children.

Finally, this book is dedicated to all the special needs children from whom a simple smile inspires us to put forth the best that humanity has to offer.

Robert A. Klingle
President, WHAS Crusade for Children Board of Directors
Vice-President and General Manager, WHAS-TV

Fifty years after the first Crusade for Children raised more than $156,000, Deimitri Miles, the 10-year-old son of Jeffersonville Fire Department Major Clark Miles, took a $1 bill from his father and handed it to someone standing in line next to him.

It was 7:44 p.m. on Sunday, June 8, 2003. The line snaked through the back lobby of WHAS-TV and into Studio H, where the 50th Crusade had been going on, both live and taped, for almost 31 hours.

What lay ahead – along with fund-raising history – was a nicely alliterative "$100 Million Moment."

Standing in that long line were firefighters, police officers, EMS workers, the very first Crusade queen, the occasional journalist, WHAS employees and many, many Crusade workers and volunteers including some who had worked each of the 50 Crusades.

The dollar bill passed quickly from hand to hand, headed toward an electronic tote board that dominated the crowded studio. The numbers on the board read $99,999,999. That dollar bill would make it an even $100 million raised to help special needs children across Kentucky and Southern Indiana.

That $100 million had provided hope and emotional support to desperate parents when both were in short supply. It offered medical help where none had seemed possible. It had made a huge difference in millions of children's lives – and would continue to do so in the future.

Waiting at the end of that long line were two of those children: Graham Maupin, 8, who has cerebral palsy, and Naudica Anderson, 7, whose eye, hearing and motor skill problems are related to cerebral palsy.

Their presence, with the blessing of the Easter Seals Center, was symbolic and especially meaningful: The Crusade for Children had its origins in televised fund-raisers for cerebral palsy sponsored by WHAS in 1952 and 1953.

They were so successful that Barry Bingham, Sr., owner of The Courier-Journal and WHAS, and station general manager Vic Sholis decided the fund-raiser had to be expanded to include the needs of all children in the Louisville area.

Fifty years later the WHAS Crusade for Children had become an event unique in the country, a fund-raising weekend that energizes tens of thousands from every part of the area to give their time and money generously – residents who patiently endured hundreds of road blocks where firefighters stood in rain, sunshine or slop holding rubber boots to be filled with donations.

Well, mostly patiently, anyway.

That willingness and generosity were perfectly illustrated with the presence of two large, very determined men standing beneath that $99,999,999 figure – Highview Fire Department chief Rick Larkins and Highview Crusade co-ordinator Bill Nord.

With a department of roughly 50 members, Highview had historically used every fund-raising invention available, including balloon rides and tool auctions. The department raised $75,000 in a golf tournament and twice helped to raffle off houses. For the sixth straight year, Highview had raised more money than any of the other fire departments, which numbered nearly 200.

THE ONE HUNDRED MILLION DOLLAR MOMENT

Crusade recipients Naudica Anderson and Graham Maupin embrace at the 50th WHAS Crusade for Children press conference.

The Crusade has been affectionately called the Boots and Buckets Brigade due to the almost 200 fire departments across Kentucky and Indiana that help raise money each year.

Thousands attended the Crusade Great Reunion where a ceremonial ribbon-cutting took place to officially kickoff Crusade 50.

Under Larkins's leadership and Nord's enthusiastic, affable and emotional persistence, Highview increased donations from $60,000 in 1993 to $435,635.29 in 2003.

Which just happened to come within that $1 bill of the $100 million mark. "I have to slow down next year; I'm killing the guys," said Larkins, who didn't seem to mean it.

Nord said he already was working on plans for the 2004 Crusade. "Everything we do is legal," he said, "but sometimes it scares me to death until I clear it with our attorney."

But volunteer firefighters had long since taken the lead in the Crusade, raising about 55 percent of that $100 million over the years. They had been doing so since 1956, when Pleasure Ridge Park Volunteer Fire Department chief R.K. Back turned in $400 and challenged other departments to do the same – or better. Fund-raising in Kentuckiana hasn't been the same since.

As the $100 Million Moment approached, and that last dollar bill moved down the line toward Larkins and Nord, it briefly touched the hands of Jeffersonville resident Ted Throckmorton, who was volunteering for his 50th Crusade.

His eyes moistened as he watched the dollar head toward an empty money box in front of the Highview firefighters – a money box representing the huge fishbowl that held the first donations a half-century ago on a hot, crowded stage at old Memorial Auditorium.

"No one," Throckmorton would say, "could have imagined it would all lead to $100 million in donations."

Finally the well-traveled bill reached Naudica Anderson, who quickly burst forward on her walker and dropped it into the box. As the bill fluttered down, the Crusade Combo played "One Dream – One Heart," the anniversary anthem.

The room swelled with fierce applause, and tiny cannons blew confetti in a bright, sparkling cloud above the BellSouth telephone operators who had been answering calls on the pledge lines.

With tears in his eyes, Throckmorton walked over to singer Judy Marshall, who was participating in her 47th Crusade. The moment was bittersweet for Marshall. The night before, she had sung at a special Crusade 50th anniversary concert in an almost sold-out Whitney Hall, featuring magician Lance Burton – who grew up in Louisville – the Neville Brothers and Kenny Rogers.

Marshall had sung the song "Smile" in honor of her fellow singer and long-time Crusade friend Jo Ann Hale, who had recently died. Photos of Hale appeared on a huge overhead screen as an emotional Marshall sang "...smile though your heart is breaking..."

"It was the hardest thing I have ever done," Marshall would say.

So on this 50th anniversary night, as almost everyone in the room was caught up in the emotion of the moment – and the sense of witnessing history that filled the place – Throckmorton and Marshall hugged for a long time. Tears flowed down Throckmorton's cheeks.

Only a handful of people had been there for all 50 Crusades. One was Milton Metz, the Louisville media legend. Metz, a fixture of WHAS-TV

Members and family of Highview Fire Department prepare to hear their final total.

WHAS-TV news anchor Jean West interviews station manager and Crusade Board of Directors President Bob Klingle during the Crusade Saturday night performances.

50-year Crusader Milton Metz stands on the side with WHAS-TV employee Mary Roush waiting his turn on the show.

and radio, was one of the four people honored for being part of all 50 shows.

The 2003 Crusade telecast opened with Metz announcing the acts – and with a tape of Metz opening the 1963 show, which included Homer and Jethro, and June Valli.

"Once you get into a Crusade it gets into your system," Metz said. "You never failed to be touched."

The vintage stars and personalities Metz worked with and around for the Crusade began with Pat O'Brien, Pedro Gonzalez Gonzalez, Hal LeRoy, Steve Lawrence and Eydie Gorme, Garry Moore, Gretchen Wyler, Lee Marvin, Jonah Jones and Cab Calloway. Later on came John Davidson, Doc Severinsen, Della Reese, The Captain and Tennille and Ricky Skaggs.

Metz said one of his toughest years came early in the Crusade when it seemed like a good idea to interview some inmates from the Kentucky State Reformatory who had come to the studio to give money.

"I was called in the next day," he said, "because some people were upset that I had interviewed a guy who might have robbed six banks and then given $12 to the Crusade."

He remembered the great University of Kentucky basketball announcer Cawood Ledford as being such a humble man that he preferred to work the Crusades wearing an apron and serving food in the basement.

He remembered – with laughter – Eydie Gorme's explaining that she and Steve Lawrence had stayed married so long because "in all that time we've never had a serious conversation."

"Every year, when you get to the studio for the Crusade, you get inflated with excitement," he said. The untold wealth that goes into the fishbowl for the children is ever exciting. The very informality of it... it's you, and us, and we're all together.

"There's plenty of room for tears as well as laughter."
Not only would the Crusade pass the $100 million mark in 2003 – with almost every penny of that given to hundreds of agencies, hospitals and schools to help children in Kentucky and Southern Indiana – but it also raised $6.3 million in donations in 2003. It was another single-year record – about 40 times the amount raised in the first Crusade.

That fund-raising came in a 12-month odyssey of the tried and true methods, not to forget the inevitable creative techniques that bordered on the wacky.

The Colgate-Palmolive Co. sponsored a run-walk that netted $8,000. Fully grown members of the McMahan Fire Department belly-flopped into a wading pool at $5 a splash, and sold "Firehouse Barbecue Sauce" for the same. Two employees of a Dairy Queen in New Albany, Ind., jokingly allowed themselves to be handcuffed to the roof of the building until they raised $1,200 – but got some revenge by being armed with water balloons.

The seven branches of the Jefferson County clerk's office held cookouts to raise almost $36,000. A male firefighter in Henryville donned a Hawaiian outfit that included two coconut shells in strategic places more befitting the opposite sex. Dozens of companies turned in money collected all year from vending machines.

Students and staff of the Hazelwood Center get ready to make their donation at the Crusade Home of the Innocents remote.

Representatives from Jefferson County Public Schools in Kentucky present their Crusade donation.

Milton Metz greets PRP Fire Chief Ernie Bohler in 1963

McAlister's Deli of Louisville turned in $21,000 just from patrons' tips. The Coca-Cola Co. began selling special commemorative bottles. Kentucky state employees turned in $77,891. The Greater Clark School System in Indiana added $4,229.50

Louisville resident George Pike ran his total of aluminum cans collected for Crusade money to an astounding 130,141 pounds – more than 65 TONS of crushed aluminum he had hauled to the recycling center himself, mostly, in a battered old car.

A motorcycle club in South Central Kentucky held the incongruously named "Touchstone Energy Motorcycle Poker Run" – and the 375 participating bikers from nearly a dozen states raised $6,517.

Despite a troubled financial year, the Archdiocese of Louisville's churches came through again, contributing $214,679. The Kroger Co., its employees an always-steady force in raising money for the children, added $117,842.32.

Bramer Custom Design of Louisville sponsored a golf tournament at "Cowhalla Golf Course" about 50 miles southwest of Louisville – a course quite literally, if not lovingly, carved from a rock-strewn hillside pasture. Some 32 semi-crazed golfers paid $35 each to pound golf balls over, around and through cow pies – new and old – in a cold, driving rain. With accompanying raffles and pasture prizes, the tournament made $4,000 for the Crusade.

Crusaders went forth across Kentucky and Indiana in clown uniforms, running shoes, bowling shoes, dancing shoes and firefighter boots – many of them going door-to-door.

Children held bake sales and hobby-horse races. Adults collected copper wire. Auxiliary members of hundreds of clubs held bake sales, dances and quilt raffles across Kentucky and Southern Indiana.

This being its 50th birthday, the Crusade sponsored a Crusade Reunion at Waterfront Park, with four bands performing old and new songs for thousands of alumni.

The surprise visitor among them was Mickey Minshall, who had been named the first Crusade Queen in 1956.

Beating the "American Idol" craze by almost 50 years, Minshall won the title as a 14-year-old New Albany resident after singing a Judy Garland song – "Inbetween" – on a live talent contest television show hosted by WHAS-TV's Sam Gifford.

Minshall brought her still golden trophy to the reunion – and to the WHAS studio on the $100 million night.

"It was a very exciting time," said Minshall, who went on to host a children's television show in Evansville, Ind. "In those days the Crusade held a big dinner at a local hotel, and you would never know who you would sit next to.

"After I found my table, the gentleman next to me pulled out my chair so I could sit. Then he held out a hand and said, `Hello, I'm Cassius Clay.'"

That tradition of dinners, live entertainment and nostalgia was evident at the 50th Crusade celebration as WHAS-TV's Randy Atcher also was remembered at the Crusade variety show.

Atcher was 83 when he died in October 2002. For many years he was a staple on Louisville television, joining partner "Cactus" Tom Brooks on the

The Kroger Company involves employees and their families when they make their donation to the Crusade.

Local television legend Randy Atcher performs on Crusade 48.

Mickey Minshall is crowned the first Crusade Queen in 1956.

T-Bar-V Ranch children's show.

But Atcher also was very much involved in the Crusade. He often provided a spiritual message with opening songs and recitations he would deliver on a darkened stage, bringing tears to the audience at home – and in the studio.

His final recitation, delivered for the 2002 Crusade, delivered to the tune of "Amazing Grace," went like this:

If you should help some little child
To walk again someday
Just imagine what a thrill
To see him run and play
Life would be worth all the cost
No matter what you pay.
If you should help some little child
To walk again someday.

"Randy was always very touched by children," said his wife, Betty Blankenbaker Atcher. "He was a very sentimental, soft-hearted person. He really loved people and loved children better than anything. He felt good that he could become part of something that could really help them. That was important to him."

Atcher was not alone in feeling the power of the Crusade, what it could do for children. At the conclusion of his act at the 50th Crusade variety show, legendary country singer Kenny Rogers pledged $1,000 to help some little child walk again someday.

It was a pledge heard across the area – if not the world – thanks to another new addition to the Crusade lineup: a multi-station television and radio network and a year-round website connection at www.whascrusade.org.

Led by the 50-year flagship combo of WHAS-TV and WHAS radio, the media network included WBKO-TV in Bowling Green, WQWQ-TV in Paducah and Murray, and radio stations WTCO in Campbellsville, WLBN in Lebanon, WRBT in Bardstown, WIEL in Elizabethtown, WHHT in Glasgow-Bowling Green, WTTL in Madisonville and WPKY in Princeton.

In addition, WHAS-TV and the Crusade established live remote broadcasts in towns around Louisville and Southern Indiana to allow fire departments to stay closer to home in the event of emergencies.

For the Sunday broadcasts, a WHAS helicopter carrying a photographer and meteorologist Reed Yadon allowed remote broadcasts from Corydon, Ind., Pendleton, Elizabethtown and Bardstown – as well as Shelby and Grayson counties in Kentucky. Some of these broadcasts were carried live on local cable stations, freeing up the WHAS studios to handle more fire departments.

That was important. All day on any Crusade Sunday – and often well into Monday morning – a flexible, well rehearsed, organized chaos reigns inside the WHAS-TV studio.

In its 50 years the Crusade had become an institution, as regular as Christmas or the Fourth of July, continuing to grow and prosper in the ten years leading up to the 50th anniversary parties.

Photojournalist Josh Grimes at the control panels during the Crusade Saturday remote show.

Members of Lafayette Township celebrate their donation to the Crusade at the Corydon, Ind. remote location.

This young Crusader sits on a bag of money while waiting his turn at the Bardstown, Ky. remote location during Crusade 50.

In 1994, with Brenda Lee in the house, the Crusade raised $3,948,732, helped in no small part by a Star Trek Club of donors featuring the usual collection of interesting androids and flat-nosed aliens. More earthly help came – as it did every year – with $100,000 from General Electric's Appliance Park.

Crusade expenses in 1994 were low – only 3.96 percent of the total raised – a continuing theme of the event. Included in that figure was money for the Theatre Authority Fund to cover union obligations.

The usually cryptic Crusade records revealed that in 1995 Tammy Wynette was labeled "one of the worst entertainers" in Crusade history by being totally uncooperative, refusing to plug the Crusade at any time during her appearance and refusing to sign autographs or make a post-appearance Crusade pitch. "Besides that," the official Crusade record said, "her singing was terrible."

Somewhat balancing out that circumstance may have been members of the LaGrange Fire and Rescue Department, who managed to flag down a very slow-moving freight train and get 50 cents from its engineer.

In 1995, the ever-energetic Redmen Club of New Albany raised enough money to put it over the $1 million mark in total donations. In the end, however, the Crusade raised $4,076,078.

Just a few days before the 1996 Crusade, tornadoes – which had become a far too common occurrence in the fund-raising season – ravaged Bullitt County. Yet by sharing the cleanup duties, and continuing with Crusade road blocks, very busy volunteers raised a record $4,948,324 for children.

Floods were a terrible problem in 1997, but the Crusade had another record year, easing past the $5 million mark at $5,027,800. It was the first year that the Belo Company, the new owner of WHAS-TV, was in control at Crusade time. Not only did Belo promise continuing support, but it kicked $54,000 into the Crusade till.

In August of 1997, WHAS radio, then owned by Clear Channel, announced it was leaving its longtime home at Sixth and Chestnut streets – in the building it shared with WHAS-TV – for new digs among other Clear Channel properties off Newburg Road. But the radio station promised continued support – and held to that promise.

With Kentucky native Ricky Skaggs and his bluegrass band providing Crusade thunder, the 1998 Crusade raised $5,508,243, pushing the 45-year total to $71,742,000. Could the $100 million mark be far away?

That was also the year that Fred Wiche, longtime WHAS-TV newsman, Crusade helper and garden guru, and one of the most beloved media figures in Louisville history, died after a long battle with cancer. Several thousand dollars were pledged to help children in his honor.

The 2000 Crusade became, in part, a tribute to Bud Harbsmeier, who retired as its executive director after a 19-year-run that began in 1982. It was another record year, with $6,067,040 in donations.

Harbsmeier's replacement was Dan Miller, a Louisville area native who had worked his first Crusade in 1973 as a Fern Creek boy scout. He had worked on the Fern Creek Volunteer Fire Department while in high school and in college.

He became an intern at WHAS-TV in 1982, working his first Crusade there in 1983. He was named the station's program manager and oversaw the Crusade

Employees of General Electric's Appliance Park announce their donation using a little creativity.

(l-r) PRP Fire Chief Doug Atwell and Todd Schindler of Lafayette Township pose with Crusade recipient Graham Maupin at the 50th Celebration press conference.

WHAS-TV's Chuck Olmstead shares a Crusade story with Crusade Co-host Terry Meiners.

show, becoming its executive director in 2000. Clearly this was a man who had seen the Crusade from both sides of the fireman's boots.

"But the Crusade is a living, breathing animal that's on the air for more than 36 hours," he said. "You're never fully prepared to take over."

Miller did get the benefit of a greatly increased Crusade staff, including marketing director John Blim; office manager Connie Dant; marketing assistant Katina Whitlock; administrative assistant Yvonne Rhoads; and business manager Donna McDonald.

With that staff came an understanding that the Crusade – as successful as it has become – had to develop a new endowment fund to keep it going another 50 years, and longer. An endowment would cover all expenses involved with the Crusade, freeing up more money for the children. And the Crusade couldn't depend on one television station to keep it afloat forever.

"Who knows what television will be like 50 years from now?" asked Miller. "WHAS may or may not be at Sixth and Chestnut or may not be owned by a company that wants to continue the Crusade.

"This year we had about 198 requests from agencies totaling $10.6 million, and we have $6.3 million to give out. What if we had a bad year economically, or the weather was really bad, and we raised only $3 million. Those agencies depend on us, and an endowment would help."

Bob Klingle, WHAS general manager and president of the WHAS Crusade for Children Board, echoed Miller's statements. He said he could not see Belo ever losing interest, but the Crusade still needed to be a more independent entity.

"The Crusade is too important to the community to change it," said Klingle. "Our own employees would probably revolt if we changed it. But on the other hand it's a six-million-dollar business and it needs to stand more by itself. This will ensure that the Crusade will be here for many generations to come."

Klingle said the Crusade's goal is to launch a $10 million endowment drive separate and distinct from the annual fund-raising drive. The drive includes a "Walk of Fame" sidewalk around the WHAS studio building, with engraved bricks selling for $100 and $500. The campaign also would include a black-tie endowment dinner and this Crusade history book.

"What we want to do," he said, "is to make the Crusade even stronger."

The changing of the guard from Harbsmeier to Miller also included bringing in WHAS radio personality Terry Meiners to succeed retiring emcee Wayne Perkey. Both would work with WHAS-TV anchor Melissa Swan, who joked she had "two Crusade marriages."

Swan had grown up watching the Crusade at her grandmother's house. She believed its amazing mix of entertainment, fund-raising and the reading of donors' names to be "the strangest program I ever saw."

And nobody has ever accused the Crusade of being riveting, go-for-broke television. In fact, many television experts who have heard about it without witnessing it, or being part of it, have declared it too corny, too dull, so prone to human error that it would never work. Which it hasn't done for nearly 50 years.

"Who knows why it works?" said Swan. "It's larger than any of us. It works because it's part of growing up around here."

As she spoke, Swan pointed to a nearby television set airing the Crusade.

1954-2002
WHAS Crusade for Children 49 SM

Always the comedian, Crusade Co-host Terry Meiners poses with Okolona Fire Chief Rich Carlson.

WHAS-TV Anchor Melissa Swan is always amazed at the dedication of fire departments. In this picture she is introducing South Dixie Fire Department Sergeant Norman Houglan.

WHAS Radio Personality Terry Meiners and WHAS-TV's Melissa Swan have co-hosted the Crusade since 2000.

A fireman reading a list of names of people who had donated – and Crusade volunteers who had died – had to pause in his reading, choked up by the emotion.

"You just don't see that in this day and age," she said of the volunteer. "People take great pride in collecting money for the Crusade."

Meiners, a lifelong Louisville resident who combines his co-host responsibilities with being the Crusade cut-up, had a serious and thoughtful answer to why the Crusade works in spite of occasionally presenting some of the most boring television imaginable in a supercharged electronic world:

"Because the core of every human being is about goodness, and the Crusade for Children every year brings people back to the center and makes us realize we're just here as part of a chain to pull each other through hardship in life.

"Everybody in this community has been touched by the Crusade in some capacity."

Everybody in a lot of communities has been touched. Thousands of adults across Kentucky and Indiana who have seen children born with serious lung, eye or brain injury have also seen their tiny sons and daughters being made well by hospital equipment marked with the "Crusade for Children" logo.

Among the most familiar – though not recognizable – faces at the 50th anniversary belongs to Dave Dumeyer Jr., whose profile has appeared on the Crusade logo for almost all of those years.

The profile was drawn by his father, Dave Dumeyer, who has been part of all 50 Crusades. In fact, the son, now living in Jackson, Miss., had returned to Louisville to be with his father for the anniversary.

"It's a pretty anonymous fame," said Dave Jr., laughing a little bit, "but it's always been great.

"I remember as a little kid working the Crusades, getting Cokes for people at the old Memorial Auditorium, so I've been involved for many, many years.

"I still have that original artwork."

His father, 80, had been hired as a staff artist at WHAS in 1953. His first Crusade job had been to find transportation for the stars as they moved in and out of town. The 50 years just sort of followed after that.

"Now I'm sort of the official greeter," he said. "I greet all the special gift people that have been given a special time to come in with their donation or contribution. I meet them at the back gate and make them feel welcome.

"I think it's a great thing to be doing the Crusade all these years. I'd hate to miss one."

His favorite memory of the early years was the day he and Vic Sholis picked up singer Mel Torme at the airport. Sholis had Dumeyer drive by Memorial Auditorium so Torme could see the theater. Torme saw he didn't get top billing on a sign outside the auditorium, and threatened not to perform. Dumeyer said Sholis found a cure for that:

"Sholis reached over, tapped me on the shoulder, and told me, 'Mr. Dumeyer, just drop me off at the TV station and take this gentleman back to the airport.'

"By the time we got to the TV station they had worked it out. So Torme

Dave Dumeyer, Jr. poses beside a profile of his head that is recognized by Crusaders around the world as the official WHAS Crusade for Children logo.

In this picture Cab Calloway is greeted by Vic Sholis and Jim Walton.

Young Crusaders with the Charlestown, Ind. Volunteer Fire Department are wowed when they see themselves on studio television monitors.

went on and performed, but he still didn't get his name on top."

Sholis also was at least indirectly responsible for Dumeyer's using his son's profile as the now very familiar logo. In the first years of the Crusade several youthful profiles were used as logos. In 1956 Sholis went to Dumeyer and requested he draw a profile, get it copyrighted and be done with it.

"It so happened at the time that my son was four," said Dumeyer, "and I had some good profile photos of him, so I thought, 'What the heck, why not?' So I used him."

Dumeyer the artist used a profile to represent the Crusade.

To flesh out the Crusade, it helps to know the moments and memories that add up to miracles. Here are some of them:

Abby Fife's work with the Plymouth Community Renewal Center at 1626 W. Chestnut Street in Louisville can be traced to a young man who needed tutoring, a young man full of hope and promise, who needed just a little more help to get into college.

"I couldn't find anyone to help him," she said, "so I decided that when I retired I was going to start an educational program myself.

"And the more I got into it, the more I realized there were other problems."

Fife, 80, had already devoted a long career to education, including being a principal at Eastern High School. But that wasn't enough. She'd come to realize that behavioral problems in school often are rooted in emotional or physical problems, such as dyslexia. She wanted to help found a tutoring center where failure would not be accepted, where children from across Kentucky and Indiana could get help.

She received her first Crusade for Children grant in 1987 – a grant that's been renewed ever since. The Plymouth Center has helped almost 6,000 students complete high school – many of whom went on to a college degree.

"I have a motto in my office," said Fife. "It says 100 years from now, no one will remember who I was, or how much money I had. But the world will be a little different because I made the difference in the life of a child."

By absolute definition, the Crusade exists to help departments such as the WHAS Crusade for Children Neonatal Intensive Care Unit at the University of Louisville Hospital – and no one is more happy about that affiliation than its director, Linda Smith.

"The entire unit," she said, "is a direct result of the Crusade."

It's in units like that – and in other hospitals in Kentucky and Southern Indiana – where the generosity of the Crusade is literally written on the walls, among other places.

"We have preemies born at 24 weeks on up," said Smith. "We have a lot of moms that have not had prenatal care, so their babies are obviously at risk.

"We do deal with a big drug population, too, so those babies are sometimes born addicted, and we have to take them through that withdrawal. So every baby in there has special needs."

Beginning in 1995 with grants of more than $1,000,000, University Hospital was able to create specific light and sound environments to allow babies born at 24 weeks to continue a life cycle as if they remained in their mothers' wombs. Children born weighing two pounds – and less – now have a chance to live because of the Crusade.

Crusade Recipient Xena Fahey, from Down Syndrome of Louisville, a Crusade funded agency, prepares to take the stage at the Kentucky Center during Crusade 50.

A Miracle Dancer, Claire Wice, gets the finishing touch before her performance on stage in the Whitney Hall.

(l-r) McMahan Fire Chief and Crusade Board member Paul Barth stands with Crusade Chief Fire Coordinator Joe Bowman and McMahan Assistant Chief Kyle Rieber.

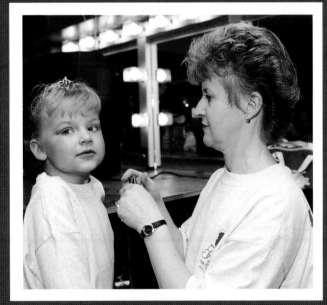

"The ones who always amaze us are the 24-weekers," said Smith. "The ones that are very, very fragile, very small.

"There's a new piece of equipment called the Giraffe. It's a combination warmer and isolette. So what you do is put these tiny infants in this warmer and you never have to move them because when it's time for them to go to the isolette, a protective lid comes down and the warmer functions as an isolette. What you do is save the infants the stress of having to move them. That piece of equipment is $35,000 and the Crusade purchased six of them for us. They're fantastic. I could just go on and on about the Crusade."

Smith said the neonatal unit creates its own family atmosphere. Nurses and staff rarely transfer from the unit. Milestones in the babies' lives are celebrated – including birthdays. Over the years, many of those babies – and their parents – come back for visits, living proof of the wonder of the Crusade.

"The staff really does bond with the families," she said. "They really do become very close, but they're also happy when it can be a situation where the baby can go home with mom and dad and be healthy.

"We have families that come back six, seven, some 18 years later," she said. "We see them graduate from college and some of our staff go to their weddings and birthday parties. They stay close. It's a very cool place."

If there is one story that illustrates what the Crusade can do to change lives, it belongs to a young man named Patrick Henry Hughes.

Born in 1989 without eyes, and a very rare syndrome called ptergyium, which keeps him from extending his limbs, Hughes is now a straight "A" student in the Jefferson County School system. He speaks fluent Spanish and often appears at Crusade functions in his wheelchair, singing his own pep song, "Crusade Cannonball."

Patrick's father, Patrick John Hughes, was a volunteer firefighter and Crusade volunteer at the Buechel Fire Department when Patrick was born – so he knows firsthand the length of the Crusade's reach.

That included visually impaired pre-school services for his son, day-care services, a special Braille notebook, talking calculators and talking computers. Patrick's goals include going to college somewhere near Nashville to be closer to country music, and perhaps make it a career.

"I have a few careers in mind," he said. "A country music singer, an international Spanish interpreter, a comedian or a food critic.

"There's only one problem with being a food critic," he said. "Nearly every restaurant I go to is, 'Hummmm… this is good.'"

In 2002, the Crusade sent $41,000 in grants to special education programs in Adair County, Ky.; $17,600 went to children being treated in Rockcastle Hospital in Rockcastle County, at the edge of the Appalachian Mountains.

Western Kentucky University in Warren County received $14,000 to provide scholarships for teachers preparing to work with special needs children. Lincoln County schools received $5,389.69 for special education classes. In Indiana, Lifespring Mental Health Services received $2,500; South Harrison Community Schools received $14,399 for children; and the First Chance Center in Orange County got $40,000.

In Louisville, more than $1 million went to Kosair Children's Hospital;

Specially trained teachers work with special needs children at Frankfort's PUSH Early Childhood Development Center.

Patrick Henry Hughes always brightens the room with a dynamic smile and performance of the "Crusade Cannonball"

10-year-old Ashlyne Scott demonstrates an assistives technology toy in the Assistive Technology Room at Cardinal Hill Hospital in Lexington, Ky.

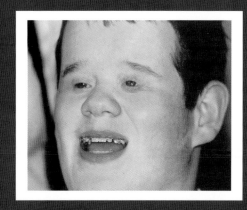

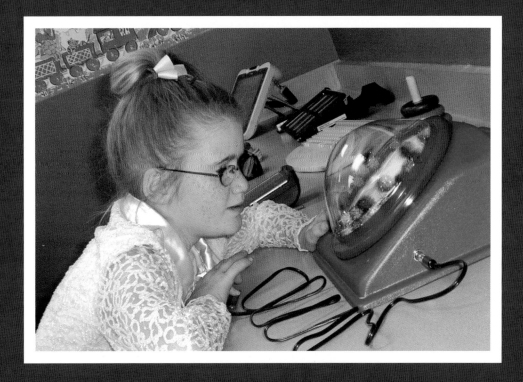

$693,000 went to the University of Louisville School of Medicine; and $3,500 went to the Kentucky Center for the Arts for its children's programs.

The main factor that keeps the Crusade so trusted – and respected – is that the grants are given out by the Crusade Advisory Panel, about a dozen rotating members from a cross-section of the Kentucky and Southern Indiana religious community. All are members of the WHAS-TV program "The Moral Side of the News."

The TV program began in 1950, somewhere near the birth of television, making it one of the longest-running local TV shows in the nation. With its panelists making the tough decisions – and there are always millions more in requests than money to fill them – panel members ask tough questions, and will gently argue among themselves before fulfilling grant requests.

It's a system that has nicely adjusted itself over the years. The panel, in effect, must estimate before each year's Crusade how much money it will give away.

Grant applications are mailed in January and are due back in early March. In the rest of March and April three rotating members of the panel hear pleas for grant requests.

After the June Crusade, and the amount of money raised is known, the panel meets one more time to disburse requests – but often with a rough idea before-hand of how much money might be available, based on the previous Crusade numbers.

Any county in Kentucky or Indiana whose Crusade volunteers raise, say, $40,000, can expect $40,000 back in grants to agencies serving children in that county.

Harrods Creek Firefighter Rhonda McDonald poses with Special Olympian Justin Huber.

Those agencies often will tell the Crusade fund-raisers how much they need, and then help raise it. Those agencies might never be able to raise that money on their own, but the power of the Crusade makes it possible.

"It's often amazing," said Dan Miller, "how often the requests and the amount raised in each county are the same."

The WHAS-TV news set becomes the Crusade Money Room where volunteers sort and bag coins by the tons.

The fund-raising is a year-long event – and in recent years wills have proved to be a big, if uncertain, source of funds – but the really big money show comes on Crusade Weekend, as it did in 2003.

Some fire departments, such as the one in Milltown, Ind., like to be first. As usual, the Milltown firefighters had beaten the rush by bringing in money to the variety show the night before, as did representatives from PNC Bank. Early Sunday morning, as is its custom, the Woodford County Fire Department made its appearance; then its members got home in time to cut the lawn.

Members of the Jefferson County Sheriff's Department volunteer their services each year during Crusade Weekend.

As the Woodford Countians tended their lawns 60 miles away, thousands of other firefighters kept pouring into downtown Louisville. They drove their big red and lime-colored trucks down Sixth Street and into the WHAS parking lot, with sirens going full blast – a screaming, intruding, reverberating presence that is felt as much as it is heard. Money is hauled into the studio by the ton, literally. It arrives stuffed in rubber boots and cloth bags. The children – and grandchildren – of the volunteers sit cross-legged before the adults as long lists of donors are read on the air.

Then, on live television with family watching at home, the children happily

dump all that money into the Crusade money boxes. They will remember those moments, and someday bring their children to the television station amidst screaming fire trucks to keep the Crusade spirit alive. A special crew of volunteers – all of them proudly wearing "Crusade Hernia Award" pins – hauls the money to a police-guarded counting room where it is unceremoniously dumped into large bins, separated by cash, coin and check, then put back in bags.

It is a crowded, noisy room operated by very practiced, efficient people who come to see the millions in cash and coins as just a commodity, something to be bagged up and hauled away in a Brinks truck, or a white, very nondescript semi-trailer.

One of the volunteers, Shay Paulin, has been a Crusade volunteer 37 years, 20 of them in the money room.

"It makes me feel good that I'm doing something for somebody," she said. Fairly new to the 2003 money-giving process was the Louisville Fire Department, which had raised $75,000, well up from the $53,600 raised in 2002.

Traditionally the Louisville department had left the Crusade fund-raising to its suburban brethren, but with the merger of Louisville and Jefferson County into one entity, the city firefighters pledged to get more involved.

More than 4,000 people will pour through the WHAS building on a Crusade weekend and wait for their television time in its cavernous, bare cement basement. It is a noisy place, filled with milling children and adults sitting on folding chairs waiting, waiting, waiting – sometimes for hours.

The basement ceiling is so tall it easily accommodates a basketball goal, which is in steady use. At one table near a mammoth elevator, Crusade volunteers assign numbers to waiting fire departments, providing best estimates about when they go on the air.

Off in another corner, near the steps, long-time volunteer Debbie Billingsley was in charge of feeding the 4,000 volunteers. It was a task made a little different in 2003 with the presence of almost 30 barbecue cookers outside the building at Chestnut Street and Armory Place.

The monster cookout – which sent clouds of hickory-scented smoke billowing across downtown Louisville – was co-ordinated by Bill Bayersdorfer of Willie B's Gourmet Smokehouse and Paul Masterson of Masterson's Restaurant. In all, 22 tons of food was fed to Crusade volunteers and distributed to agencies across Kentuckiana.

Other parts of the 2003 Crusade were just as pungent, poignant, memorable and bizarre – if not frightening. Here are some of the author's recollections:
• Briefly standing in the middle of a very busy Dixie Highway with Pleasure Ridge Park Fire Department Capt. Roger Milliner collecting money as cars blew past during the green lights, continually missing Milliner and fellow volunteers by inches.

"I do it because it's kind of a good thing for the community and the kids," said Milliner, leaning away from a passing car. "Besides, I'm a very competitive person."
• Seeing the Saturday night Whitney Hall performance of the "Miracle Dancers," members of the Diane Moore Dancers who gracefully performed in

Jason(l) and Jody(r) Meiman take a break from orchestrating fire department volunteers to pose for a picture.

The Crusade collects several tons of change each year.

The basement of WHAS-TV becomes a "Crusade Wonderland" with tons of food, drinks, games, and activities for the thousands of volunteers that enter the building during Crusade Weekend.

wheelchairs as the Roger Dane Orchestra played behind them, bringing many in the audience to tears.

• Watching two brothers, Jody and Jason Meiman, and many members of their family, tearfully accept the Crusade's "Buddy Award" given posthumously to their father, Ed, who had worked the Crusade for 35 years. Then the brothers went back to work helping the Crusade.

• Watching two and three tons of money getting stuffed in bags, then placed on carts where a volunteer shrink wraps all the loot to keep it from falling off a cart. Then the money was casually hoisted, by forklift, into a truck. Imagine what would happen if that load spilled someday?

• Listening to children describing what they had done, the hours they had spent, to raise money for other children.

• Listening to so many people say they were involved with the Crusade not because their children were ill, but because they were healthy, and they appreciated that enough to want to help those who needed it.

• Anticipating that moment that occurs every year when the Crusade money is all but counted, another year is over and there is little left to do but be thankful, and, of course, have everyone still standing after another 36-hour marathon sing "God Bless America."
As in:

God bless America,
Land that I love.
Stand beside her, and guide her
Through the night with a light from above.
From the mountains, to the prairies,
To the oceans, white with foam,
God bless America, My home sweet home.
God bless America, My home sweet home.

The Diane Moore Dancers curtsy to a standing crowd in the Whitney Hall of the Kentucky Center.

Crusaders celebrate the closing of Crusade 48 in 2001.

But when all was said and sung, it was Buddy Head, a LaGrange, Ky. firefighter who best summed up the enduring mystery and wonder of the Crusade. Head, a Crusade volunteer for 47 years, now helps co-ordinate television coverage of the Crusade for units for Oldham, Henry, Trimble and Shelby counties.

He's seen it all in those 47 years, watched the Crusade grow, adapt and change, watched the donations climb from $200,000 to $6.3 million. Can it keep going, he was asked. Can the Crusade raise ever-increasing amounts of money, continue to find support, be there forever to help future generations of children?

"I don't think it can," said the veteran Crusader, "but it does."

The miracle of the WHAS Crusade for Children began in 1952 with a meeting of concerned parents in the basement of Louisville's Heyburn Building.

The first Crusade as we now know it was still two years away – on Oct. 16, 1954. The 1952 meeting brought together parents of children born with cerebral palsy. Frustrated because they had nowhere to go for medical help and emotional support, they had formed United Cerebral Palsy of Kentucky.

They would work with a man named Orman Wright, 28, who had a background in voluntary health work and Louisville journalism before joining the Kentucky organization.

"We needed to raise money," Wright remembered. "They had solicited a few donations here and there, but we didn't have any money."

Trying to solve that problem, Wright made contact with the national United Cerebral Palsy organization in New York. The first thing its executive director suggested was a telethon – a television show to raise money. Wright had one major problem with that: "I had never heard of a telethon and I don't think anyone else in Louisville had either."

Telethons – if not television – were in their infancy in the early 1950s. It was all live, black and white, and tentative. In fact, Wright was dubious about holding a telethon in Louisville. The executive director briefly explained the process: Hire a few stars, get a TV station to stay on the air for 18 to 20 hours and raise money by asking viewers to make pledges, or better yet, invite them down to the show to give money in person.

"That doesn't seem like a very effective technique to me," Wright told the executive.

"Well," the executive answered, "it is."

Wright went to New York and got a crash course in telethons – how to recruit volunteers, how to line up the facilities and show business stars he would need. Then he returned to Louisville to meet with the parents' group.

"About 40 to 50 of them showed up," he said. "I gave them a briefing on my trip to New York, told them we needed to get started and unless there was some urgent reason why they couldn't, I was going to start the next day."

Wright first stopped at Louisville's WAVE-TV, Kentucky's first television station. Wright said he spoke with the program manager about hosting a telethon for United Cerebral Palsy of Kentucky, but WAVE wasn't interested. Wright next stopped at the office of Ralph Hansen, program manager at WHAS-TV.

"Ralph was very interested," Wright said. "We had lunch together at the Brown Hotel, had a few drinks, spent the better part of an afternoon together."

As the men parted, Hansen said that before a decision was made he had to reach Vic Sholis, the station's vice-president and general manager. Sholis was out of town, working on Adlai Stevenson's presidential campaign. Wright waited a few days, then called Hansen back. No decision had been made – Hansen said he had been unable to get in touch with Sholis. Wright and Hansen agreed to meet again for lunch.

"After lunch we went back to Ralph's office in the old WHAS offices atop the Courier-Journal building," Wright said. "Ralph was able to get through to Sholis. Ralph cocked the receiver over so I could hear the conversation, and Sholis said, 'Ralph, you're the boss, dammit, go ahead and make the decision.'"

HISTORY, PROMISE AND ZIPPY THE CHIMP

"So Ralph said, 'Okay, Vic.' They said goodbye and Ralph turned to me and kind of grinned. He said, 'We're going to do it.' I said, 'Okay.' So we did it."

The men decided the first telethon would be in the autumn of 1952, barely a month after the phone call to Sholis. Wright said teams of volunteers began contacting fire departments, police departments, women's clubs and service clubs seeking support. He arranged to rent Memorial Auditorium at a nominal fee to serve as telethon headquarters.

Wright then called the national United Cerebral Palsy headquarters in New York, asking about the stars to host the telethon. A week later the executive director called back with a question:

"How does Rosemary Clooney sound?"

"That sounds great," said Wright.

"How does Garry Moore sound?" the executive director added.

"That sounds great, too," said Wright.

It was more than great. It was close to the telethon jackpot. Kentucky native Rosemary Clooney was on her way to becoming one of the country's biggest stars. Garry Moore was a popular TV star. The two would literally set the stage for following Crusade for Children events, which would feature dozens of famous actors, actresses, singers and performers lined up across the stage of the venerable auditorium.

The pair was mobbed by autograph seekers greeting the train at Union Station. Then it took a police escort to get them to a line of cars waiting to parade them through town to the Courier-Journal building – where the eager locals swamped them again.

Clooney was radiant with her shimmering blond hair and broad, girl-next-door smile. Moore, bringing along much of the entourage from his TV show, displayed his trademark bowtie and crew-cut hair. That night star-struck Louisvillians stuffed Memorial Auditorium, lining up on its front steps beside a welcoming sign that promised an "ALL NIGHT TELEVISION SHOW" at the CEREBRAL PALSY "Parade of Stars."

The show was scheduled to begin at 10:15 p.m. Saturday and last until 2 p.m. Sunday – a brief, by modern Crusade standards, 16 hours of television. Technicians from the United Cerebral Palsy organization in New York came to Louisville to show WHAS-TV cameramen how to set up and deliver the best shots.

One of the people there that night was Mary McCawley, now 87. She had helped organize United Cerebral Palsy of Kentucky as an effort to help her young son, Pat.

"Rosemary Clooney and Garry Moore were real troupers," she said. "By Sunday morning not much money had come in so she went back to her room, changed clothes and came back and went right on singing and cajoling people."

That first year was a learning experience for everyone. Organizers wanted live auctions. So telethon volunteers had to go out and ask local merchants to donate anything from refrigerators to lamps to a cause they knew nothing about – and to a telethon with no track record of success.

"But they did it," McCawley said. "I guess they trusted us."

It was her husband, "Mac" McCawley, who started a tradition that would

The accounting department worked in the basement of Memorial Auditorium tabulating the totals on adding machines.

In the early stages of the Crusade volunteers from Southern Bell worked at long tables in the basement of the auditorium.

Zippy the Chimp was one of the more unusual guest stars to appear on the Crusade.

become synonymous with the Crusade. Wanting to have children – and adults – parade across stage to give money on live television, Mac McCawley went to Haller's Pet Shop and borrowed a huge fishbowl for the proceeds.

More than 300 telephone operators from Southern Bell staffed 90 phones in three shifts to take pledges. Also starting a tradition, the Yellow Cab Co. took United Cerebral Palsy representatives to the homes of people who pledged more than $25 – a big chunk of change in 1952 – to pick up the money. WHAS-TV's Jim Walton emceed the event, beginning another tradition that would carry well into the first 50 years of the Crusade.

Orman Wright remembered something else from that first night that would become the heart and soul of the Crusade: firefighters bringing in donations, helping the children.

"They were not as organized at that time," Wright said, "but there were a lot of firemen there. The kids had made collections around their neighborhoods and they would come up to the stage and drop money into the tank, and we would give them a reward, a little plastic bank shaped like a baseball on a pedestal."

For all that, the mood had turned a little glum when donations for the first few hours totaled only $13,400. A trash fire beneath the stage shortly after midnight sent about half the crowd of 3,500 filing out for a while, and didn't much help the evening.

"We were really upset," Mary McCawley remembered. "We wondered if it would be a success or not. Then Sunday morning the money really started coming in."

During the two telethons for cerebral palsy – and in the early years of the Crusade – many of the handicapped children sat on the stage in front of the audience; they would often walk across the stage to meet the hosts. McCawley said their son, Pat, then three years old, was the first child ever to walk across a telethon stage in Louisville.

"We stood next to him and then his dad let him go," she said. "We held our breath and he made it across the stage."

To the utter amazement and delight of everyone involved, that first United Cerebral Palsy of Kentucky telethon raised $115,000. Its leaders had set a tentative goal of $75,000, but had no real idea what to expect.

Buoyed with that success, a second cerebral palsy telethon was held in 1953. The featured stars were singer Mel Torme, dancer Ray Malone, antic comic Pedro Gonzales Gonzales and Warren Hull of television's "Strike It Rich," who co-hosted the event with Jim Walton. Local celebrities Randy Atcher and "Cactus" Tom Brooks added to the charm.

The effect was exhilarating. Show officials estimated at least 25,000 people would visit the show, some to watch the entertainers, some just to bring donations. By Sunday afternoon the line into Memorial Auditorium stretched all the way around the building – much of it excited children with parents in tow, wanting to drop money in the fishbowl, then be seen at home by grandma or grandpa watching television – if they had one.

More than 5,000 baseball banks were given away, and the show was extended 45 minutes – which would become another tradition – to get everyone

Employees of WHAS-TV and WHAS Radio created an in house studio and production area at Memorial for the radio and television broadcast of the Crusade.

Early Louisville television pioneer (l) "Cactus" Tom Brooks from the T-Bar-V Ranch Show was among local celebrities who would appear on many Crusades.

into the building. Soldiers and civilians at the Armor Center at Fort Knox contributed $5,000.

Foreshadowing the magic of the Crusade for Children – and the incredible and enduring generosity of the area – The Courier-Journal reported, "Scores of churches collected special telethon offerings. Gifts came from Baptist ministers and bartenders; from bankers and bookies; from policemen, firemen, attorneys, businessmen, unions, poker parties, and physicians. The East End Democratic Club contributed part of its bingo proceeds. One WAVE-TV employee gave a week's salary."

The 1953 United Cerebral Palsy show raised about $170,000, more than anyone could have imagined. That level of success was quickly noticed by Vic Sholis and Barry Bingham Sr., the president of WHAS-TV, WHAS radio and The Courier-Journal. Those two powerful men also noticed that 25 percent of the money received – after expenses – was going to the national United Cerebral Palsy organization, which had been very much instrumental in getting the telethons going in Louisville.

So, according to both Orman Wright and Ralph Hansen, Sholis and Bingham decided to broaden the scope of the telethon to include all physically or mentally handicapped children in the Louisville and Southern Indiana area. The fund-raising would include both WHAS-TV and WHAS radio; the money would go to specific projects serving handicapped children and would be in addition to the health organizations' regular programs.

No money collected could be used to replace an organization, and none could be sent to a national headquarters for any purpose, or to defray an organization's general operating costs. The huge appeal of that plan was that all money raised here would stay here. The very word "telethon," in fact, had begun to have a bad connotation across the country because so much of the money pledged was never collected, and a large percentage of what was collected often left the area. Both Bingham and Sholis were determined that would not be the case with the new WHAS fund-raising drive for children.

"It will be," Sholis said in a Courier-Journal story, "for a broader community purpose."

By all accounts Sholis could be a tough man, who would and could back visiting celebrities into a corner, even offer them an early plane ticket home if their egos got in the way of raising money for the children. It was Sholis who decided to call the money-raising efforts "The Crusade for Children" – borrowing a word from Dwight David Eisenhower's victorious presidential campaign over the man Sholis had worked for, Adlai Stevenson.

The decision to launch the Crusade greatly affected the fund-raising abilities of United Cerebral Palsy of Kentucky – which had lost its telethon – but did allow for the Crusade to reach into many more areas where children – and parents – needed help.

From Day One, Sholis and Bingham also guaranteed the enduring and sustaining credibility of the Crusade. They mandated that panel members of the WHAS-TV program "The Moral Side of the News" would listen to presentations from health organizations from Indiana and Kentucky requesting funds, and make all allocations.

That first panel included Dr. Duke McCall, president of the Southern

Audio engineers work in the corner of the stage at Memorial Auditorium.

This picture taken during Crusade 4 shows the new location of the Southern Bell volunteer phone operators on the stage in 1957.

As the Crusade grew, more volunteers were needed to track the phone pledges. This busy "make-shift" accounting department was beginning to fill the basement of Memorial Auditorium.

Baptist Theological Seminary; the Rev. Felix Pitt, secretary of the Catholic School Board; Dr. Frank Caldwell, president of the Louisville Presbyterian Theological Seminary; Dr. Joseph Rauch, rabbi of the Temple Adath Israel; and the Rev. Robert Weston, pastor of the First Unitarian Church.

Let the record show that the opening act in the Oct. 16, 1954, Crusade for Children was WHAS singer Bill Pickett and the Atherton High School chorus, offering the prophetic "A Great Day's A'Coming" – with 50 years of entertainment to follow. Jim Walton again emceed the television show, but this time he was joined by WHAS radio personality Bud Abbott on the vocal side, along with Mary Snow Ethridge.

The show was scheduled for 15½ hours, from 10:30 p.m. Saturday night to 2 p.m. Sunday. Headliners included Pedro Gonzalez Gonzalez, who was back by popular demand, along with actress Monica Lewis, dancer Hal LeRoy, singer Bill Hayes, Don DeFore of "The Adventures of Ozzie & Harriet," and actor Pat O'Brien, who also promised to do a song-and-dance routine.

Ever the gentleman and patrician, Barry Bingham Sr. promised the TV and Memorial Auditorium audience the show "would benefit children to whom nature had not been very kind."

Hundreds of members of the Bingham media empire's "family" helped as volunteers, collecting and counting money, answering phones and serving donated food. Louisville baseball legend Pee Wee Reese also took time to answer phones and raise money.

Those were less socially conscious times, and many of those children sat along the stage, some wearing beanies promoting "The Crusade for Children," their crutches and wheelchairs nearby. A group called the Day Camp Rhythm Band, sponsored by the Society for Crippled Children, noisily rehearsed with cymbals, tambourines, bells and triangles backstage.

They were also more innocent times. Seated in the audience that night were Al and Carolyn Basham, a Louisville couple now married almost 50 years, who were on their first date that night.

"I was living with my sister and her family at that time," Carolyn Basham said, "and I had a little bitty old record player that broke.

"Al worked for Baxter Radio and Television Repair on Baxter Avenue and my sister worked with him. She knew him. When I got home from work that night she told me Al was coming over to fix my record player.... And the record player never got fixed."

Instead, the couple rode in Al's pale green 1949 Ford to the Crusade, parked on Fifth Street, stayed at the show from the opening number until after midnight. Then they went to Frisch's on Third Street for a hamburger.

"What caught me about the show was the little kids walking out there on their crutches and the people with them just had them take another step," Carolyn recalled. "That really got to me."

The Bashams were married on Oct. 7, 1955, less than a year after the show. They had four sons, who all became active in the Crusade, two of them as members of the Pleasure Ridge Park Volunteer Fire Department.

"Is there any other one?" asked Carolyn Basham, laughing.

She said her son Tim had once been collecting at road blocks and at homes

for 24 straight hours, came home to take a nap with blisters on his feet and his face all sunburned, only to have another fireman show up and pull him out of bed.

"Come on, Tim," the fireman said, "We got to go."

Former WHAS-TV employee Bob Pilkington also attended that 1954 event – and hasn't missed one since. In the early years he orchestrated the opening four hours and wrote some of the accompanying pledge pitches. That would include some camera direction – and WHAS was using four TV cameras inside Memorial Auditorium, twice the number in the company studio – and making sure the manually operated tote board got plenty of air time.

With most of the stars coming in on Friday, attending a big party that night, then hitting a 9 a.m. rehearsal on Saturday in preparation for the show, there was little sleep for anyone the entire weekend.

"My goal," said Pilkington, laughing, "was to survive."

He remembered Pat O'Brien's having pretty much the same attitude. Crusade officials had been warned that O'Brien liked his whiskey, and when he arrived in Louisville, Pilkington said, "they poured him off the plane."

O'Brien also had a wee bit of trouble answering interview questions, but showed up for rehearsal the next day ready to go, and was more than a saint as he soberly raised money for needy children.

O'Brien would also be credited with getting the Archdiocese of Louisville more involved in the crusade, rallying the Catholics to the cause after watching yet another Protestant minister drop money in the fishbowl.

"Where are all the Catholics, the Knights of Columbus, the priests, the nuns?" he shouted – and they've all been loudly heard from ever since.

Much of the music in the early Crusades was provided by the WHAS Crusade Band, remnants of the 18-piece ensemble that once provided live music for radio and television broadcasts. One year, Pilkington's brainstorm was to bring the trombone players from four or five high school bands and have them join the Crusade band's trombones in a rousing version of "Seventy-Six Trombones" from "The Music Man."

"I had this very intricate pattern worked out," Pilkington said. "You do this, then so many steps. You do that, then so many steps. I mean those guys did high school football games. They ought to know that.

"They got out there, they hadn't rehearsed, and I mean to tell you it was the god-awfulest mess you ever saw in your life. They all wound up facing front at the end, and that was about the best thing you could say for it. But it was fun – and I didn't do that anymore."

For months before the Crusade show, WHAS-TV would air programs featuring the handicapped children. Pilkington went to some of those shows and found inspiration for his audience "pitch pieces."

"I would come in from my office and stand in the corner and watch the kids until I couldn't stand it anymore," he said. "Then I'd go back in my office and write in a frenzy.

"I remember one year we had Lee Marvin as a Crusade guest and he came off the stage after reading one of my pieces and he asked my wife, who was backstage keeping the log, 'Man, who wrote this?'

"My wife said, 'My husband did,' and Marvin laughed and said, 'Well,

In this photo, members of Pleasure Ridge Park Fire Department make their donation to the Crusade. PRP fire department was the first fire department to collect for the Crusade in 1956.

Actor Pat O'Brien is seen here posing with a group of ladies at the Seelbach Hotel. O'Brien is credited with getting the Louisville Archdiocese involved in the Crusade.

Monica Lewis and (r) Actor Don Defore who played "Thorny" on "The Adventures of Ozzie & Harriet," visit the volunteers in the accounting department.

you tell him if he writes any worse he could go to Hollywood.'

"I got kinda ticked off until, you know, after seven years or so I began to think maybe he meant it as a compliment."

Near the end of his production years with the Crusade, Pilkington put together the "Big Finish" for the show – a montage of emotional moments, funny moments, the tote board flashing success, perhaps a sunset and, of course, a few hundred people crammed on stage singing "God Bless America" as tears rolled down cheeks across parts of two states.

Pilkington does not remember who first suggested singing "God Bless America" – it may have even dated to the United Cerebral Palsy shows. He does know he wants to be a part of the Crusade for Children as long as he can.

"It's a feeling you get can't anywhere else or any other time of the year," he said. "It's a cumulative thing. I mean those of us who have been doing it for many years just wouldn't give it up."

The first Crusade for Children had a goal of $200,000, but the total raised was $156,725.92. Crusade organizers vowed to do it again in 1955 – but never again announce a set goal, to prevent disappointment on all sides. The Crusade gave out 20 grants with the 1954 donations, including $21,728 to United Cerebral Palsy of Kentucky; $15,000 to construct a kindergarten at the Kentucky School for the Blind; and $22,930 for work in children's mental health, one of the first such programs in Kentucky.

The Crusade steadily picked up steam all the way through the 1950s – although donations usually hovered around the $200,000 total. The 1955 show was moved to September – and would remain in September until 1969, when it was moved to late May. The Bingham media empire's employees continually volunteered to help. They included artist Ben Ramsey, who put together a WHAS Crusade for Children coloring book, and the great political cartoonist Hugh Haynie, who would draw hundreds of cartoons for the children.

Bingham continually encouraged the Crusade, with promotions in the family newspaper and on radio, including pitches from Ronald Reagan, Gene Autry, Jackie Robinson and Ann Landers.

The 1950s celebrities included Don Cherry, Eydie Gorme, Rosemary DeCamp, Bob Keeshan ("Captain Kangaroo"), Cab Calloway, Steve Lawrence, Jonah Jones, Homer and Jethro, Richard Simmons (TV's "Sgt. Preston"), Buster Crabbe, Tommy Leonetti, Lee Marvin and, yes, Zippy the Chimp.

Of all those guests, Zippy the Chimp caused the most lodging problems. According to Louisville Times columnist Al Aronson, Zippy was signed up for the 1956 show after Vic Sholis and Ralph Hansen went to New York to recruit talent. They noticed a big crowd on a street corner.

Wondering what could draw any type of crowd in blasé New York, the two men moved closer to see Zippy luxuriating in the back seat of a cream-colored Cadillac convertible, along with another chimpanzee named "Snow" because of the color of his pelt.

A little investigation brought Sholis and Hansen in contact with Zippy's owner, Lee Ecuyer. The men signed up Zippy – and Ecuyer – for the Crusade and booked them rooms in a luxury Louisville hotel, the Seelbach. But hotel

Academy Award winner Lee Marvin offers his services for the Crusade in 1959. Marvin spends Crusade Sunday assisting the money carriers with moving heavy fish bowls of cash. At the end of the Crusade, he donates his pay check back to the Crusade.

(c-r) Jim Walton and singer Tommy Leonetti pose for a picture at Memorial Auditorium in 1954.

(l-r)Tommy Leonetti, Jim Walton, and Lee Marvin soak their tired feet in buckets of water after enduring a long Crusade 6.

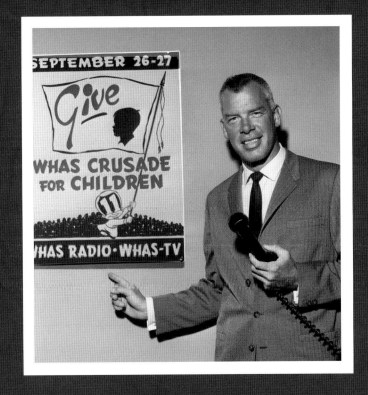

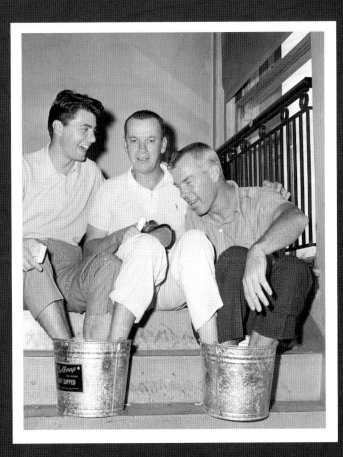

management refused to book a chimpanzee, and Zippy moved to a motel.

Ever the trouper, Zippy recovered nicely, put on a great show and was even photographed making a (non-singing) appearance in the "God Bless America" finale.

On a more serious note, the incredible timing and planning involved in putting on 16 straight hours of entertainment was evident in a 1950s program guide given to all participants.

The show opened with Mary Snow Ethridge reading from a script on the reason for the show. The script now reads on the melodramatic side, but its message was as powerful as it was emotional:

"I would like to speak to you of children. I watched a thin little boy come towards me, his hands gripped tightly on the walking bars which helped his arms bear his weight. He was eight years old and sweat stood on his brow as he tried desperately to make the muscles in his legs respond to his desire to walk.

"He was like every other eight-year-old, except for two legs that could not walk. His effort was painful for me, as well as for him. I yearn to reach out to help him, but I knew this must be his accomplishment."

The show moved from there to orchestra music and a mention of the guests.

Then emcee Jim Walton explained what would happen over the next 16 hours – a time when almost everyone involved would get little sleep.

Walton introduced Barry Bingham, then each member of "The Moral Side of the News," with each speaking briefly. He gave the TV audience two phone numbers for pledges: JACKSON 3261 and CLAY 6611. Money could also be wired via Western Union to: "CHILDREN, LOUISVILLE, KENTUCKY."

Then, in a grand flurry of music and fuss, each of the Crusade celebrities would be announced and walk quickly to a phone, ready to take a pledge from a viewer eager to speak directly with an Eydie Gorme or Lee Marvin.

By 1956 the Crusade had added pledge centers in Lexington, Frankfort, Elizabethtown and Bardstown. U.S. marines volunteered to ride in Yellow cabs to pick up pledges: It would be really hard to say no to a marine. Crusade records indicate 1956 was the first formal appearance of the Pleasure Ridge Park Volunteer Fire Department. Its $400 donation would be followed by millions more over the next 50 years. That same year WHAS-TV and the Crusade held their first King and Queen contest. It was a talent contest in which entrants tried out during the WHAS-TV "Hi-Varieties" show hosted by Sam Gifford, with the eventual winners crowned King and Queen of the Crusade.

Already showing the geographical reach of the Crusade, the 1956 winners were Lee Dean of Harrodsburg, Ky., and Mickey Minshall of New Albany, Ind. Perhaps the most interesting sidelight to the popular King and Queen talent contest was the girl who didn't win. Her name was Diane Sawyer, of 29 Sterling Road. She was shown in a 1960 Courier-Journal photo as a preliminary winner and was mentioned as a finalist in 1961. Her "talent" was listed as singer-monologist – the latter paying a few dividends as she went on to some national fame in television.

Long, long into the night and early morning the celebrities would take 15-minute shifts giving live performances, clowning around, answering telephones – all acts of will, ability and kindness that would seem hard to find in celebrities

Jim "Mr. Crusade" Walton enjoyed the smiles of the children helped by the Crusade.

1961 Crusade Queen Sherry Sizemore and King Bill Haas. Sizemore would perform on many Crusades with singers Jo Ann Hale and Judy Marshall.

Local celebrities(l-r) Randy Atcher and "Cactus" Tom Brooks join future "Days of Our Lives" star Bill Hayes.

today. Part of their function also included being a part of the "Parade of Beanies" when hundreds of children, their parents, and all talent would parade around in their blue-and-white Crusade beanies, which were given away by the thousands as souvenirs.

All the work, the fun and the children are vividly remembered by Phyllis Knight, who became one of the first women to anchor radio and television shows in Kentucky. She worked the 1955 and 1956 Crusade shows on radio, then switched to television in 1957. Her memories of Memorial Auditorium in May remain vivid – especially its basement, which was lovingly nicknamed "The Black Hole of Calcutta" because of its dim interior and the steady clumping of dancers on stage overhead.

"It was HOT!" Knight said. "That auditorium was not air-conditioned and the toilets all overflowed. The women had such a time because in those days we wore long, formal dresses and you had to hold your dress up."

Knight well remembered Jonah Jones because the Louisville native loved to perform in his home town and be with family. As an African American, he had grown up in a segregated Louisville and learned to play with the Booker T. Washington Community Center Band.

"We put all our performers up in the Seelbach," said Knight. "Jonah said as a child he was afraid to go into the Seelbach because he wasn't allowed, and here he was being treated royally."

Photographs of the Crusade participants – performers as well as guests and children standing in the lines – showed a strong determination by Crusade officials to include all parts of Louisville.

A headline in the Aug. 30, 1962, Louisville Defender – the community's African-American newspaper – said "Two Negroes Are Winners in Crusade Contest for King and Queen."

The list of proposed talent for the 1950s Crusades stretched all the way from Phil Silvers, Red Skelton, Eddie Fisher, Pat Boone and Doris Day to Sammy Davis Jr., Louis Armstrong, Nat "King" Cole and Eddie Anderson ("Rochester" of "The Jack Benny Show").

After her appearance, singer Eydie Gorme wrote a letter to The Courier-Journal. It said:

I understand that the WHAS Crusade for Children is on the very brink of success. With approximately $172,000 on hand and some 3,000 pledges yet to be filled it isn't unthinkable to think in terms of $180,000.

Even this is not too much when the cause is handicapped children of every religion and race in your community. I urge everyone who has pledged money to fulfill that pledge so those wonderful ministers can put Crusade funds to work. It was a thrill for me to be with you in this great effort. Please accept my sincere thanks and congratulations.

EYDIE GORME

Phyllis Knight and Jim Walton try to keep Crusade fire hats from toppling to the ground.

Volunteers provide coffee, cold drinks and food in the basement of Memorial Auditorium.

"Stephen Foster Story" performer Jay Willoughby takes a moment to entertain children sitting on the Crusade stage.

Knight said some of the performers were paid as much as $10,000, but others came because CBS – the network WHAS belonged to in those days – made them come, and paid their way.

"However, they would come with their girlfriend or boyfriend, their music director, and all of them first class. Most of them thought they were big stuff." Part of her job was to meet celebrities at the airport. Most got here without any trouble. Some, including 1959 guest "Peg Leg" Bates, had some difficulty.

"He lost his airplane ticket, and, of course, he had a wooden leg. When he got to the airport they said, 'Can you prove who you are?' Here he is, standing there with a wooden leg."

Knight praised the many "local" stars who joined the show each year, men and women like Judy Marshall, Jo Ann Hale, Mary Anne Luckett, Mel Owen and his orchestra, Pee Wee King, Karen Kraft, Carl "Tiny" Thomale, Grady Nutt, Dean Shepherd, the Red River Ramblers, Pete French, Ange Humphrey, The Monarchs, Dr. Tim Stivers, and Monica Kaufman, who would go on to TV anchor fame in Louisville and Atlanta.

A man named Nelson Keyes wrote "The Crusade for Children March" to be played as the children paraded across stage to dump their money into fishbowls. Band director Jack Crutcher, after three bouts with eye surgery, wrote new arrangements for the Crusade's 18-piece band and 40-member orchestra by dictating notes to a 16-year-old helper. WHAS-TV film director Charles McDaniel would spend five months preparing almost 700 volunteers to work in 18 specific areas.

"It's family," Knight said of the Crusade. "It's just family. People we see only once a year, the fire department from General Electric, people from the archdiocese, all the contributors, they would walk in and we would hug and kiss. It was family time and I don't know that you would find many TV shows that are that way."

Sometimes the happenings on the always crowded stage area got a little too cozy, such as the night Sam Gifford, Knight's husband, got hit in the face with a fishbowl.

"The one thing I remember about Vic Sholis is he was always sure we had fishbowls," Knight said. "One night Vic came out on the stage, put his arm around me and said, 'Now, don't panic, but Sam's been hit in the face with a fishbowl and it broke his nose.'

"But we had a doctor on hand. We always had a doctor in case something like that happened."

Knight said the Crusade was always trying new ways to raise money, one being to organize over-the-road truck drivers to contribute. It didn't raise a lot of money, but it did get her a CB handle – "Big Mama."

Knight and her Crusade family found moments when the work of thousands of volunteers became intensely personal.

"Nine years ago my granddaughter almost died," said Knight. "When my daughter walked into Kosair Children's Hospital and on the bed it said 'A gift of the Crusade for Children,' my daughter just lost it. She just cried and cried and cried.

"But this has happened to so many people, and the people who volunteer

(l-r) Singer Tommy Leonetti, dancer Peg Leg Bates, musician Charlie Shavers and singer Tina Robbins are greeted at the airport by WHAS-TV's Vic Sholis.

Jazz legend Cab Calloway speaks to a Louisville women's group before his performance in the 1954 Crusade

After his astounding tap performance using a prosthetic leg, Peg Leg Bates talks to Crusade MC Jim Walton.

their time, like so many of the firemen, are very grateful people. When you do something for them, they appreciate it. They knew when the article came out in the paper telling how much money we had and how much we had spent, it was the truth."

Sex almost raised its ugly head during the 1958 Crusade, when Gretchen Wyler joined Bobby Hackett and the Billy Williams Quartet as featured stars. Wyler had brought only one costume, but it so tightly wrapped her amply endowed frame that she wasn't allowed on live television until after it was deemed the kiddies had gone to bed.

An almost universal memory of the 1959 Crusade was of the Hollywood tough guy - and somewhat tipsy - Lee Marvin needing about 18 takes to record a promo correctly, then becoming so enchanted with the Crusade he did everything from performing with great charm to carrying money. It rained that weekend, but Marvin insisted on going out and shaking hands with every wet volunteer fireman he could find.

When the Crusade ended, Marvin endorsed his check and gave it back to the children.

That was also the year "Tarzan" actor Buster Crabbe worried aloud what he could do since he couldn't sing, dance or juggle.

"Well, if I fill the orchestra pit with water," Vic Sholis asked him, "would you jump in and drown?"

In 1959 the Crusade raised $197,372.13 with expenses of only $15,106, or 7.6 percent. Over the years Crusade officials have consistently taken pride in the fact that so little Crusade money goes to expenses, and they work hard to keep it that way.

Ever mindful of Pat O'Brien's message to the Catholics, the Archdiocese of Louisville was again the top giver with $24,655.84 donated – although area fire departments had already begun to challenge one another and would soon take over leadership.

By then Crusade officials were sure to count money from Indiana and Kentucky separately, and would return the money in kind. Crusade centers had been set up in almost a dozen Kentucky and Indiana cities – a precursor to the 21st Century Crusade, which would reach into most Kentucky counties and a broad portion of Southern Indiana. Care would be taken that money donated from those areas would go back to those areas, too.

Most important, by the late 1950s the Crusade was helping 35 child-related agencies in areas of mental health, rehabilitation, hearing and physical and mental disabilities.

The 10th Crusade for Children was held Sept. 21-22, 1963, and featured hillbilly comics Homer and Jethro dressed in clothes more reminiscent of a jail break, and then wearing Corn Flakes boxes on their heads. It would raise $289,095.69, with the money given to 45 agencies. It was also the first year money had been left to the Crusade in a will; Susan McLeod of Woodford County gave $5,000 through her volunteer fire department.

Wills would become a continuing source of Crusade money. And the Archdiocese of Louisville was still the top donor, giving $33,229.81. But by then almost 70 fire departments from Palmyra, Ind., to Columbia/Adair County, Ky., were regularly making donations to the Crusade. So were dozens

McMahan Fire Department reports its Crusade collection during Crusade 5 in 1958. McMahan is known for its white fire trucks, a tradition started in 1955.

"Moral Side" Panelist Monsignor Felix Pitt addresses the Crusade audience.

of local businesses and organizations.

Newspaper clips from the early 1960s told of Louisville Mayor Bruce Hoblitzell's promoting a water ski thrill show on behalf of the Crusade. The group with the most interesting and enduring name in Crusade history – the Improved Order of Redmen, Manzanita Tribe No. 276 – conducted fund-raising drives in New Albany in full headdress.

The Scottsburg, Ind., Volunteer Fire Department set a bathtub out in the road and asked people to fill it. Thirty hard-working St. Matthews children held a play in a back yard and raised $7.49. In Frankfort, Ky., American Legion Post No. 7 held a youth parade fund-raiser. About 400 women went house-to-house in Frankfort at the same time seeking donations.

A shopping center in Jeffersonville, Ind., sponsored a carnival. The Adair County Volunteer Fire Department had road blocks. Col. Harland Sanders took time off from fresh broasting chicken to give $2,000. Four small girls in Beechwood Village held a fashion show with their Barbie dolls and raised $12.

The Courier-Journal would publish full-page stories each year detailing where the money had gone, maintaining community trust in the cause: $5,000 for the Washington County, Ind., Council for Retarded Children; $15,175 for the Kentucky Department of Mental Health; $2,000 for the Floyd County, Ky., Council for Retarded Children.

In time, a Crusade pattern developed that would last 50 years; the bulk of the contributions needed to push contributions ahead of the previous years always came at the very end, and then, at least in those early years, accompanied by a giant shower of balloons from the Memorial Auditorium ceiling.

Louisville Times writer Dudley Saunders wrote of the 10th Crusade: "The 18-hour-and-five-minute telethon was a real nail biter during the last few hours when a lot of us – especially the newcomers – were beginning to wonder if the money was ever going to arrive.

"The suspense started building about breakfast time when we realized the Crusade was more than $200,000 shy of last year's receipts.... The suspense was so great that June Valli, Johnny Johnston, Henry "Red" Allen and Homer and Jethro risked missing their planes by sticking around long after they had made their final appearances."

Then, Saunders wrote, the "cavalry" arrived in the form of "several thousand volunteer firemen who started pouring in about noon, their fire-fighting boots and flashy helmets overflowing with money."

Courier-Journal television and radio critic Bill Ladd also wrote of those phenomena in a column that holds true to this day. After 10 years, the Crusade had grown up, become uniquely and wonderfully ingrained in our community fabric. There was nothing else like it in the country. Nothing.

"It's a strange experience living through one of these Crusades," wrote Ladd.

"When the performers show up for rehearsals on Saturday there is sort of an apathy among the out-of-town talent. This is another grind, another telethon, and they act as though they had been shanghaied aboard.

"The local boys and girls have a different outlook. They have been through the Crusade before and they know what to expect; that the people of Kentuckiana will respond and everything will come out in the end.

Vic Sholis and Phyllis Knight celebrate the 10th anniversary of the WHAS Crusade for Children with a cake in 1963.

Local star "Cactus" Tom Brooks entertains singer June Valli before she takes the stage.

"As the night hours drag on and the tote board seems anchored, some of the visitors become discouraged. You will find them slipping off to the hotel for a bath or a nap.

"About 9 o'clock Sunday morning, things begin to wake up. The church pledges start. The kids begin to line up outside for the parade past the fishbowls. The firemen begin to call and the filled boots begin to arrive.

"Suddenly everyone comes alive. The local actors will find the out-of-town folks at their side, asking for work, begging for the mike and making pleas for money. Those who are not working go through the audience collecting money and signing autographs. Others ask for the assignment of going out on the street to wave to the passing cars and take donations.

"There is the smell of success mingled with the perfume and deodorants and the makeup. Collars are loose, ties discarded, shoes unlaced and shirts sticking to sweaty torsos.

"The enthusiasm which has kept Jim Walton, Randy Atcher, Tom Brooks and the whole local crew 'up' all night now takes everyone by storm.

"At last it ends. The cast is reluctant to leave the stage. They go to a hotel room and live these last hours over again. And ever after, if you meet one of these performers in New York or Hollywood and say, 'I'm from Louisville,' the guy's eyes brighten up and he says, 'Boy, I remember I was there on a Crusade.'"

Randy Atcher enjoys a moment with one of his adoring fans.

Jim Walton poses with a young boy wearing a leg brace during the 1954 Crusade for Children.

"Cactus" Tom Brooks toys with 4 year old Margaret Ann Gillespie while her grandmother, Mrs. Althea Stilwell, looks on.

The second decade of the Crusade for Children began much as the first.
had ended, with tireless Jim Walton in control as emcee. Walton's radio pedigree
ran back almost to Marconi. His early years at WHAS radio included "Dream
Serenade" during which he read poetry to the organ music of Herbie Koch. He
later was the disc jockey on "Walton's Wax Works" and did the "Coffee Call"
show with Bill Pickett. He hosted the "Late Show" on WHAS-TV, which gave
him training for the all-night stint with the Crusade – a job he took very seriously.
Some of that serious work required constant verification of pledges phoned in to
the South Central Bell employees answering the phones. Walton told one funny
story about the year he resisted mentioning a $5,000 pledge on the air until it
was verified. The donor was wakened at 4 a.m., asked if he had given $5,000
and replied "hell no."

Walton also often expressed the opinion the Crusade was a unique and
uplifting look at the best we can be.

"The Crusade," Walton once said, "means too much to fully explain in
words. But I would say that it means a chance for all of us to prove our faith,
hope and love.

"The Crusade is not a program to perform as much as it is a feeling to
experience. It's a long moment when thousands of people show the part of
themselves which is closest to God. It's a time when our values come into proper
focus.

"The show belongs to others and I'm just the figurehead standing in front
of the curtain, reading pledges and introducing the people who do the work."

Among the featured acts in 1964 was The Pilgrims, a trio billed as a
"folk-pop" group and featuring Robert Guillaume, who would go on to television
fame.

"My real last name is Williams," Guillaume confessed in a television
interview, "but there are a lot of other Robert Williamses in the business.
Besides, now I'm stuck in the bottom of the alphabet."

Appearing with The Pilgrims were The Gray Sisters, five young African-
American women named Charlene, Dorene, Arlene, Rose and Mary.

Endlessly creative in getting out the message, Crusade officials also sent
out small "space fillers" to be used at the bottom of newspaper stories to fill
out a column. The fillers often were unrelated to the story above them, but
provided interesting nuggets of information to keep the Crusade name alive.
A few of them went:

"It takes four tons of equipment to televise and broadcast the WHAS
Crusade for Children each year. This includes 30 telephones, 20 microphones,
three 12-foot scaffolds and four TV cameras."

"Every recipient of a WHAS Crusade for Children Grant must submit
a quarterly report to 'The Moral Side of the News,' the panel of ministers
who are allocators of the funds."

"The volunteer workers during the 1963 Crusade for Children consumed
500 pounds of ham and beef, 7,000 cups of coffee, 175 cases of soft drinks and
600 loaves of bread – all donated by local merchants."

"Over 150 reserve marines help with crowd control at Memorial Auditorium
during each year's Crusade for Children. This same unit has been performing this
duty for eight years."

3

JIM WALTON, TOTE BOARDS AND TONS OF MONEY

Jim Walton watches as a young boy dumps his bank into the Crusade fishbowls in 1965.

"The Pilgrims", including future star of the television show "Benson", Robert Guillaume, performed on Crusade 11.

In 1961, Crusade MC Jim Walton talks with one of the children helped by donations to the Crusade. The United States Marines, like the one seen in this photo, played a big part in early Crusade broadcasts.

"The 1963 WHAS Crusade for Children radio-TV program ran 1,085 minutes and raised $266.45 a minute."

"Though donations to the WHAS Crusade for children have come from as far west as California, as far south as Florida, as far east as New York and as far north as Michigan, the funds raised are spent only on the handicapped children of Kentucky and Southern Indiana."

"One of the most unusual donations to the Crusade came in 1956 from a French poodle named 'Missy' – she gave $5."

"The 1956 WHAS Crusade for Children sponsored a hearing survey of Kentuckiana children that indicated 2,767 children required medical attention. It also found a marble in one child's ear and a screw in another's."

As helpful as that might have been, 1964 Courier-Journal stories showed the Crusade was already having an enormous impact in the community – beyond marble removal. It gave a $90,000 grant to what was then called Children's Hospital for a Crusade Heart Laboratory that could pinpoint defects in newborn infants. About $6,000 of that grant enabled Children's Hospital to buy a special heart pump to facilitate open-heart surgery in babies. It was the only such pump in Kentucky and one of only 20 in the nation. The new pump cut the delay in operating from 48 hours to 30 minutes and reduced the amount of blood required.

"The equipment functioned perfectly during an operation on a six-pound child," said Dr. W. Fielding Rubel. "With our previous equipment we were restricted to children weighing approximately 24 pounds."

The 1965 Crusade brought a pair of firsts, both illuminating in an odd sort of way. One was the sudden appearance of local "go-go" dancers in very brief costumes. The women had been collecting in their nightspot, so after defining the full reach of the Crusade, they wanted to share their $30 bounty with viewers on live TV. The director let them on, but to be shown only from the neck up, and absolutely no bending over the fishbowls.

The perhaps more illuminating event that year was the appearance of a working "tote board" from Churchill Downs, to flash the Crusade totals.

According to newspaper columnist Floyd Edwards, the apparatus was the work of electrician Louis Schueler, who spent three years adapting a tote board donated by the American Totalisator Co. of Towson, Md., for Crusade use.

"Each of the six digits that lights up with Crusade figures is operated with a separate box of components, lamps, selector switches, indicators and related electronic gear," wrote Edwards. "Schueler worked out the electrical hookup pattern to fit the Crusade board. Through the long hours of the show he nurses the devices tenderly, unseen and unsung. His company, Henderson Electric, donates the wiring and maintenance. The six electronic units have been returned to the Maryland company for use again calculating and flashing payoffs at tracks, including Churchill Downs. The control panel has been put in storage in the station studios."

Trumpeter Doc Severinsen – then billed as first trumpet in the Skitch Henderson Orchestra – was so great in 1965 he was invited back for the 1966 show. Over those two years he would share the stage with Bobby Lewis, Damita Jo, Grady Nutt, Paula Wayne and David Seville and the Chipmunks.

Children waiting in line outside Memorial Auditorium were given balloons by Crusade volunteers.

Doc Severinsen and his band performed in 1965 and 1966 on the Crusade broadcasts.

The Columbia Adair County Volunteer Fire Department joins the Crusade effort in 1963.

Severinsen's sextet, with drummer Bob Rosengarden, was joined by Louisville musicians. They jammed for hours, thoroughly rocking the auditorium.

"It's great," Severinsen said. "I've never seen or done anything like this before."

Another Crusade old-timer, Jerry Lloyd, joined WHAS in 1966 to work in production, and ended up directing a segment of the show on only two weeks' notice.

"It was like going into a jazz place in New Orleans," he said. "If you did this show twice it would never be the same because the music was different, the ad libs were different and everybody had one great time.

"A lot of people would stick around because they could end up playing with people like Doc Severinsen. There were jazz sax players, marimba players from out of town, people who would come in from Chicago or somewhere.

"You put four or five musicians like that together and you're going to have a heck of a time. So these people would end up staying until 4 in the morning.

"You know, jazz goes on until you fall off the bench."

A year-by-year history of the Crusade compiled by Malcolm Jenkins as part of a school project mentioned that in 1966 the Archdiocese had raised $38,346, but the fire department pledges reached more than $200,000. The total raised in 1966 was $415,592 with expenses of only $14,454.65 – an incredibly low 3.5 percent of the money raised.

In 1967 the Crusade was broadcast in color for the first time, creating a logistical nightmare for company crews who had to move in about 25 tons of equipment – making the already cramped stage three times brighter and seemingly 300 times hotter, requiring a double-deck row of specially constructed fans.

The change required a whole team of makeup artists from a local modeling agency. Their donated time prevented the performers' faces from looking like animated tomato cans. Thus an estimated 8,500 people walked across the stage that year in full, living color. The show lasted 20 hours and became billed as the longest live color telecast in world history – which was then not a particularly crowded field.

Augmented by about $1,500 from the work of Police Court Judge William G. Colson, who gave defendants facing minor charges the choice of paying a fine or contributing to children, the all-color Crusade raised $481,493.93 in 1967 – with expenses of only 3.4 percent. As a new record was set, balloons rained from the ceiling, and the Crusade band broke into "Hot Time in the Old Town Tonight."

Jeffersonville businessman and beer distributor Ted Throckmorton can testify to both the hard work done by the Crusade volunteers – and some of the fun that went on in the often-hot confines of Memorial Auditorium. Of the tens of thousands of people who have volunteered for the Crusade, he is one of the four left who have been to all 50.

"The 50 years have been a very high part of my life," Throckmorton said. "It's an honor and a pleasure. To me, with two healthy children and two healthy grandchildren, it's just a small payback for what God has given me in my lifetime."

Throckmorton said the early Crusades had almost a party atmosphere. There would be a luncheon Friday for the stars, then a cocktail party Friday night. Saturday morning might include a boat trip for the sales representatives,

Crusade 12 in 1965 brought the singing and dancing greatness of the "The Rhythm Kings" to Memorial Auditorium.

Ted Grubb (far right) led the Crusade Orchestra for many years, including 1963 when this photo was taken.

Henry "Red" Allen wowed the audience with his musical performance during Crusade 10 in 1963.

and Throckmorton would make sure some of his beverage was available in a discreet place during the actual Crusade.

For most of those 50 years Throckmorton worked with a woman named Carmel Cullen, a Southern Bell employee who helped organize the huge teams of volunteers who answered the pledge phones – 10 on stage and 100 more in the cramped basement.

"The girls would write out the pledge cards with carbon paper and we would have to check the pledge cards and make sure everything was the way it was supposed to be," Throckmorton said. "Then they would go into accounting, be checked there, then mailed out to the person that made the pledge."

He said a tiny woman named Frances Johnson, who would later marry legendary Kentucky broadcaster Cawood Ledford, would guide the almost 150 handicapped children who attended the show onto the stage, care for them, and make sure they got home safely.

"She would have them all scheduled," said Throckmorton. "That was a very responsible job then because they would have to meet the families in the cabs, get them in, make sure they were taken care of because it was just a constant live production from beginning to end."

Throckmorton said editorial cartoonists Allen Blankenbaker and Hugh Haynie would sit for hours and draw cartoons for all the children who took part in the Crusade. Cawood Ledford and a man named Jim Topmiller were in charge of the food – and other things.

"Cawood always came down to take a look at the phone operators and try to pick the queen of each shift," he said. "So it was a fun thing, but a serious thing, and yet, I think that everyone who worked back then when it was live enjoyed it. I had a lot of people tell me one thing about going in there – you didn't go to sleep. You stayed awake while the show was going on. If you went to sleep, a marine would come up, tap you on the shoulder and make sure you woke up and did what you were supposed to do. And that was a big-time ticket to get into Memorial Auditorium during the live show."

As a dyed-in-the-wool Hoosier, Throckmorton said he has seen a lot of things over the years that have divided Indiana and Kentucky, but the Crusade has never been one of them.

"The Crusade has always had a very, very reliable and up front accounting system," he said. "You can see where your money goes. The Southern Indiana money stays in Southern Indiana. The Kentucky money stays there.

"But there's never been a division in the Crusade itself and I think that's because of the unity of the fire departments. The men and women volunteers come together for a common cause. It just all comes together. There's just no divisions when it comes to the Crusade, or helping handicapped children."

Throckmorton said the only sad part about his 50th Crusade was that Carmel Cullen would not be there to help; she passed away about three years ago.

"We made a pact that we were going to work at least 50 years," he said. "But the enthusiasm she brought is still there. The legacy she left is very special to me."

In 1968 the Crusade, then broadcast on WHAS-TV as well as the Bingham companies' radio stations, tried a little different tack; there were no major stars

The Shively and Dixie Suburban Fire Departments bring their Crusade donations to the Crusade on stretchers in 1965.

Yellow Cab drivers volunteer to provide transportation for special needs children appearing on the show as well as pick up donations to the Crusade.

Kentucky Governor Edward T. Breathitt helps phone operators take pledges during the Crusade.

hired to lead the show, although local stalwarts Jo Ann Hale, Sherry Sizemore and Judy Marshall again were on hand, and Mel Owen was picked to lead the Crusade orchestra. The change was a success; Crusade income squeezed past the half-million-dollar mark for the first time, settling in at $538,312.64 with only $16,149.38 in expenses, an all-time record low of 3 percent.

Somehow included in that fund-raising total were Canadian, German, Peruvian and Bahamian coins and a Louisville bus token.

In December 1968, Vic Sholis and Barry Bingham decided to move the 1969 Crusade – which would be the 16th – from September to May to avoid competition with the United Way campaign, which came to a head in the fall.

The move worried Crusade officials because the 1968 Crusade had ended only eight months earlier, cutting in on the time and ways the various organizations needed to raise money.

Indeed, as Sholis announced the date change he said, "To conduct this Crusade in May 1969 – just eight months after the last one – will obviously create problems. These do not involve WHAS alone.

"Therefore we have tried to explain our reasoning and purpose to many of the groups whose devotion and generous support have developed the Crusade into the unique undertaking it is.

"It is inevitable that the change will pose some difficulties for thousands of volunteers who join us in our annual program since they are being asked to make substantial revisions in their plans and activities.

"We have such faith in the spirit which has motivated our supporters in the past, however, that we believe they will enable us to overcome the problem of changing highly successful patterns."

1969 Crusade Queen Colette Skinner waits her turn to go on air during Crusade 15.

Long-time Crusade emcee Jim Walton also was named executive producer of the show in 1969, reflecting what Sholis described as "an increasingly" complex show that needed someone to handle the advance planning, organization and presentation.

Jim Walton, Barry Bingham, Jr. and Vic Sholis on the Crusade set in 1963.

The 1969 show somewhat dipped back into the star talent pool again, signing up Bobby Lewis, Diana Trask and Hal Frazier to perform. Notable among the "local" talent that year was singer Monica Kaufman.

The 1969 Crusade comes to a close with the traditional singing of "God Bless America."

The ever-diverse Crusade selected African-American singer Colette Skinner of Winchester, Ky., as the Queen Talent Contest winner. Also performing on stage were The Voice of the Deep South, a group of six Louisville men who had been singing on local radio stations – and around the country – for 30 years.

A 1969 Courier-Journal story featured a Saturday Monte Carlo night in which the wives of Camp Taylor volunteer firefighters raised money for the Crusade. By then, Kentuckiana bowling alleys had begun to host regular Crusade fund-raisers, and the Golden Gloves boxing championships included Crusade donations. The change to May also had one unintended consequence: Several people donated winning tickets from the 1969 Kentucky Derby.

This uplifting news, however, was somewhat balanced by a Courier-Journal editorial taking Police Court Judge William G. Colson to task for having defendants fork over money to the Crusade rather than to the court system.

Indeed, Colson's unusual system had raised another $2,500 in 1969, but Barry Bingham Sr., publisher of The Courier-Journal and Louisville Times,

warned Colson the Crusade would not accept a nickel of it, saying court money should remain in the courts where it was badly needed.

Crime, however, did continue to pay for the Crusade: A 1969 Courier-Journal photo showed a Floyd County (Ind.) sheriff's deputy smashing confiscated slot machines with a sledgehammer. The $73.25 found among the wreckage was donated to the Crusade.

Other Hoosiers kept finding interesting ways to donate that year. New Albany's Greenleaf Café sponsored a nickel-a-week club for 154 of its regulars, with all the silver going to the Crusade – roughly $750.

There also was a little musical controversy in 1969 as the Doctor's Band, a group of 16 doctors, two medical students, a dentist and a businessman, didn't appear on the show as advertised when the musicians' union refused to sanction their participation. Whatever the strange mix that year, the fears of moving the Crusade date proved largely unfounded. The Crusade raised $547,719.12 – yet another record.

By then, the officially "unofficial" contest among the almost 100 fire departments raising Crusade money was in full swing. The top three finishers in 1969 were St. Matthews, $23,054; Pleasure Ridge Park, $20,605; and McMahan, $16,500.

As the Crusade headed into the 1970s – and with its 20th birthday on the horizon – some of its more prominent names began to change. With the retirement of the Right Rev. Felix Pitt, all the original members of "The Moral Side of the News," the people who decided where the money went, had retired.

The 1970 panel became Dr. John Claypool of Crescent Hill Baptist Church; Father E. John Prechtel of St. Francis; Dr. J.J. Gittleman of Adath Jeshurun; Dr. Jo M. Riley of First Christian Church; and the panel's first African American, Rev. Irvin Moxley of the Presbyterian Center.

As the money totals grew, so did the Crusade's air time. What had begun at about 16 hours for a United Cerebral Palsy telethon had crept well past 21 hours of live TV – and climbing.

Courier-Journal reporter Rick Northern wrote of the 1971 Crusade: "Arms locked, a worn and weary crew of volunteer firemen, marines, WHAS staffers and others sang 'God Bless America' a few minutes before eight last night ending the 1971 Crusade for Children, the biggest, longest and, for most, the best ever.

"The tote board said $612,147… the 1971 Crusade was on the air for 21 hours and 55 minutes, one hour and three minutes longer than last year's."

In 1973 – the Crusade's 20th year – the show went on for almost 23 hours. The headliners that year were Milt Buckner – his fourth Crusade – Bobby Rosengarden, Jo Anne Worley and "M*A*S*H's" McLean Stevenson.

That year, The Courier-Journal's John Filiatreau wrote about the truly little people who have always contributed to the Crusade magic:

"The little boy from Pleasure Ridge Park sold lemonade at 2 cents a glass for two days and netted 36 cents.

"He and some friends pooled their money and put on a show in his garage making $12.50 and incidentally doing their bit to preserve the cherished memory of vaudeville.

"The children went house to house on their block, collecting money. Then

Lake Dreamland Fire Department and Auxiliary members present their donation to the Crusade.

"Moral Side of the News" Minister and Crusade Panelist Rabbi J.J. Gittleman of Adath Jeshurun addresses the Crusade audience.

(l-r) Crusade MC Jim Walton, Archbishop Thomas J. McDonough and Vic Sholis meet once again to announce the Louisville Archdiocese total.

they went home and asked their parents for their change.

"They jammed the money – nearly 20 dollars – into an old instant coffee jar, label still attached, and carrying it like the Holy Grail, piled into a battleworn station wagon. Off to Memorial Auditorium.

"There they stood in line for nearly an hour, debating as to who would be the spokesman for the group, finally settling the argument by deciding to have three co-spokespersons. They finally gathered in a little bunch on one side of the stage, squinted under the harsh television lights, watched themselves on the monitor, chanted their names at WHAS's Barney Arnold like soldiers counting cadence, and smiled.

"Then, after a long, deep breath, the three spokespersons proudly announced their grand total – $19.73."

Louisville Times writer Howard Rosenberg, who would later win a Pulitzer Prize as TV critic for the Los Angeles Times, concentrated more on the bigger kids in his 1973 story:

"Firemen and other groups awaited their turns on stage – some of them for hours – in a large, subterranean room which was cooler than in past years, but just as jammed. The packed cavern was reminiscent of turn-of-the-century refugees arriving at Ellis Island.

"Money – tons of it – was deposited in glass tote boxes on stage and then was taken to guarded counting and separating rooms. White-gloved volunteers handed the money through the windows to armored car personnel for the trip to the bank.

"Meanwhile, Mary Flynn, a veteran of 18 Crusades, and three other volunteer nurses sat in their first-aid station awaiting emergencies that never happened. Their duty consisted of treating comedienne Jo Anne Worley's pin-pricked finger.

"A Crusade is eight parts organization, then add two parts confusion, which added together makes 10 parts exhaustion. It is saxophonist Arnie Lawrence playing until you think his lips will fall off. It is squat organist Milt Buckner and many other musicians and singers.

"It is Jo Anne Worley, a Louisville Police Department shoulder patch guarding the top of her cleavage, a long cigarette holder extending from her mouth. She enters the basement waiting room and asks rather loudly, 'Is there a fireman in the room?' Only a couple of hundred.

"It is an Indianapolis couple who drove down with a $10 contribution because it was a nice day for a ride. It was Hardyville's 200 families contributing $1,424.

"And it is McLean Stevenson of 'M*A*S*H,' the outrageous madman who passionately kisses the Crusade queen – and king, who pole-vaulted into the orchestra and landed on the piano.

"See him always with the Crusade kids, the physically and mentally handicapped ones on stage, sitting with them, patting their heads, whispering into their ears.

"But what does he say to the little blonde girl who's so shy and cannot speak or hear very well. A volunteer answers: He asked her to dance with him.

"They paid Stevenson $1,000 for coming. He donated it to the Crusade."

McLean Stevenson was a Crusade favorite. Crusade volunteers remember him most for pole vaulting over a set of drums.

Jo Anne Worley, an Ind. native, was well known for her role on the television series "Rowan and Martin's Laugh In."

Jim Walton (l) and Milt Buckner (r), an avid Crusade supporter, talk to a Crusade recipient who has also collected for the Crusade.

As the WHAS Crusade for Children headed into its third decade of fund-raising in 1974, a tornado had just devastated Brandenburg, Ky. Still, its fire department and other Meade County firefighters collected $2,356.49 to help others.

Nearby Irvington, also struck by the deadly April tornadoes that hammered Kentucky and Indiana, collected $2,161. At Hanover, Ind., where Hanover College bore the brunt of another twister, the fire department collected $2,433 with the help of nearby Madison firefighters.

Brandenburg firefighter Casey Shilton explained that about 25 town residents, many of them teenagers and younger, set up road blocks on the edge of town, and also went door-to-door in battered neighborhoods collecting money.

"The people dipped down in their pockets and gave the money," he told The Courier-Journal. "Not one said a word about their homes being wiped out in the tornado."

That 21st Crusade became notable for several other reasons.

• One was an attempt to bring a little more organization to the seething, sweaty atmosphere inside Memorial Auditorium by giving the many volunteer fire departments exact times to appear on stage. It was a noble effort, but many departments said, "Thanks, but no thanks." They didn't want to face the TV cameras until certain they had raised more money than the year before.

• The always-generous employees of General Electric's Appliance Park passed on the traditional check-giving ceremony and gave $50,000 in $1 bills.

• It would be the final Crusade for Vic Sholis, who was retiring from WHAS. He received a silver tray from Jim Walton, along with his thanks for "nursing the baby that started in 1954 and raising it to full maturity at 21."

• It would also be the last Crusade in venerable – and air-conditioning-free - Memorial Auditorium. The move to a new location became necessary in 1975 because of a strike by stagehands at the auditorium. The most likely alternative was the new – and cavernous - WHAS facility at 520 West Chestnut Street, on the same block with the other Bingham holdings, Standard Gravure printing and the Louisville Times and Courier-Journal.

"The biggest problem we'll have," WHAS-TV program director Dick Sweeney said in a Louisville Times interview, "is not knowing what problems we'll have."

Memorial Auditorium held about 1,000 people, and the WHAS studio had room for only 160, with half of that space reserved for children and their families. The move meant the end of the long lines of Crusade-watchers snaking around the building, with the more informal setup inside, and the almost casual comings and goings of hundreds of people carrying thousands of dollars in the coin of the realm.

The trade-off was cool air, better studio lighting and the prospect of smoother, more tightly organized programming. But organizers feared that the change would somehow separate the Crusade from the community, that people would lose their emotional attachment.

"If they can't walk in when they want to," Sweeney said, "it doesn't allow them that full community involvement."

Not to worry. With Phyllis Knight as the new executive director and

FIRE - FIGHTERS SHOULDER THE LOAD

Fire Departments from across Kentucky and Indiana collect for the Crusade and proudly bring their donations in for the broadcast. Children wave to friends and family across the viewing area.

This Cub Scout Troop earned a service badge by working hard to raise money for special needs children.

The 1973 show celebrated 20 years of the WHAS Crusade for Children.

producer, and with the Crusade broadcast on all the Bingham stations as well as statewide by the Kentucky Educational Television network, the 1975 Crusade raised $903,943.16 – almost $100,000 more than the previous year.

The Crusade magic had been more easily transferred than anyone could have imagined. The noise and hullabaloo of the fire trucks parked outside Memorial Auditorium, sirens screaming, was moved to Armory Place – and later Sixth Street – outside WHAS.

New sets in the new setting were provided by WHAS craftsman Harry Campbell. Food and drink would be served in the mammoth studio basement, with coffee provided by SYSCO Louisville Food Services Inc., as it had been since 1955. The Greatest Show in Fund Raising went on – despite a depressed economy and a new location.

"It's really no big deal," SYSCO vice-president Albin B. Hayes would say of the company's 42 volunteers who showed up to brew 400 pounds of coffee. "We go down to the station and do what we can. We're just doing something for the kids."

The 1975 Crusade also marked the sixth consecutive appearance by jazz organist Milt Buckner, who was becoming as familiar to Louisville viewers as thoroughbred horses in May.

No stranger to world acclaim, Buckner had played at Carnegie Hall, in the capitals of Europe, and coast-to-coast in the United States. But every year in May he would pack his organ in a van and drive down from his home in Ohio to entertain the Crusade audience. One year he flew in directly from Europe.

"I was hooked the first time I made it here," he said. "I liked the way the Crusade people operated – no politics. I'm a sucker for that sort of thing."

The 1975 Crusade would turn out to be the only one broadcast live by Kentucky Educational Television – and WHAS had to pay to make that happen. Crusade organizers had hoped the added coverage would bring in enough money to justify the added cost. It did not.

But proof that the Crusade was already having more and more impact out in the state came in the form of the largest gift the Crusade had ever received up to that time: $77,000 from the estates of two sisters, Martha and Helen Gill, of Lancaster, Ky.

By 1975, the total money given to the Crusade in its 22-year history was approaching $9 million. As impossible as it would have seemed to workers in the early 1970s, in the next 28 years the Crusade would raise $90 million more.

But raising more and more money each year also began to require a lot more co-ordination between fire departments in Kentucky and Southern Indiana – the men and women who had become the heart of the Crusade effort.

In the late 1970s that co-ordinating effort fell into the capable hands of Bill Greenwell of the Highview Fire Department. He had first become involved with the Crusade collecting at intersections.

In 1976 he assisted Middletown Fire Department chief Bob Martin, who had put together a crew to welcome firefighters to the WHAS building.

"At the time I think there was 80-some odd fire departments involved and it was getting a little unwieldy," Greenwell said. "Bob Martin left to go into business for himself and Phyllis Knight asked if I would put together the

This picture shows the new Crusade set at WHAS Television Studio H. The Crusade Sunday show is still broadcast live from the television station.

Highview Firefighter Bill Greenwell is shown here taking a break from his busy coordinating assignment to have a bite to eat.

same crew and do the same thing.

"I thought to myself, 'What am I going to do with 83 fire departments?'" The number has since grown to nearly 200.

"I still don't know what to do with them," Greenwell said.

Greenwell's job soon expanded to more than co-ordinating several hundred fire trucks for the Crusade weekend. Knight asked him if he would also serve as a liaison between WHAS and the fire departments, to get ideas and give the fire departments a voice so it would not seem as if WHAS was dictating the Crusade agenda. It was a job he would keep until the 2000 Crusade.

"We would go out year round and meet with the departments individually, and as county units, and tell them what was coming up.

"We would find out what their plans were. One thing we did initially was run a clearinghouse of sorts to keep neighboring departments, or at least departments close, from planning a function or a fund-raiser at the same time."

That co-ordinating meant Greenwell might have to tell one department holding a fish fry that a nearby department had a chicken supper the same night – and ask one of them to change the date. He kept track of all the culinary events – and hundreds of others – in three-inch binders, and served as binding arbitrator if need be.

The fund-raisers were as varied as they were successful: dances, raffles, bake sales, street festivals and carnivals. One year eager firemen went into a Seventh Street Road nightspot where the female entertainment began selling kisses for $1. Not to be outdone, the firemen began selling kisses for $1, too. But mostly Greenwell had to co-ordinate less exotic fund-raisers, and in time the departments learned to co-ordinate them by themselves.

"Hopefully, everybody that planned something would check with me first," he said. "I had notes on each department. They were all indexed and I had a master calendar."

Co-ordination was important for another reason: As one fire department headed downtown toward WHAS – sirens screaming and lights blazing – it was vital that neighboring departments were available in case of a fire.

"You can imagine what the publicity would be if a small community with maybe three trucks had all its equipment and manpower downtown and a fire started," he said. "Crusade would get the blame for it."

So the Crusade began to establish remote telecast sites closer to the outlying departments, along with co-ordinating who would deliver the money-laden boots – and when.

One year, in fact, when a tornado tore through Pioneer Village and Zoneton in Bullitt County a few days before Crusade weekend, some Jefferson County firefighters went to Bullitt County to collect money while the Bullitt firefighters worked the cleanup.

All this work was above and way beyond Greenwell's regular job as security director for Goodrich Chemical Company.

"It started out a few hours a week, but it ended up from February on becoming a 40-hour-a-week job, especially when you would get up toward the Crusade," he said.

In the early 1980s, as the co-ordinating task became overwhelming,

Buechel Fire Department makes its donation.

Members of Danville Fire Department drive almost 100 miles to make their donation the Crusade.

Campbellsville Firefighters pose for the picture before heading out to man road-blocks for the Crusade.

Greenwell set up a committee of seven area co-ordinators who would handle the day-to-day questions in their departments and counties, then report to him. Then Greenwell set up another co-ordinating committee at the WHAS end to handle traffic control and radio communications. Thus the happy invasion of siren-blowing firefighters could be handled with a degree of almost military control:

"We would put their trucks where they had to be and make sure they came across the stage at the same time their truck rolled up for a camera shot. I think we had 13 or 14 people co-ordinating all that. We had checkpoints. We set up a command post."

There were no military salutes – or secret handshakes. But no amount of organization could stifle the competitive juices between the various departments, each eager to top last year's total, if not the neighboring department's total.

In the Crusade's early years it was usually the Archdiocese of Louisville, or General Electric, that brought in the most loot. Greenwell remembered one year when the Pleasure Ridge Park Fire Department learned in advance how much the Archdiocese had collected – and found itself about $800 short of being Number One.

"The Pleasure Ridge chief had people soliciting right here downtown," Greenwell said. "They even went over to the Federal Building and were getting money out of the fountain."

Greenwell said Pleasure Ridge Park has been the only department that kept it final total secret until its members walked out before the Crusade TV lights – a secret made possible because it had five departments within the one.

"Each one of the five stations is sort of run by a captain," he said. "The captain runs the effort in each of the five, and the chief of staff co-ordinates it. No one captain knows what the other has done."

Greenwell said truth and accuracy are often not associated with a fire department's pre-Crusade declarations, either. Indeed, the Crusade often involves more sandbagging than the 1937 flood.

Greenwell remembered one year when the Harrods Creek fire chief, a good friend, was loudly complaining about what a disappointing year it had been raising Crusade money.

"Everyone keeps records as to how well they did on a Friday this year as opposed to last year," Greenwell said, "and the chief told me, 'It's not looking good. It's terrible. We went to one of the most affluent subdivisions and instead of getting $100, $150 and $200 checks, we were getting coins.'"

Greenwell said he was practically depressed at his friend's rotten luck. Then came Crusade Sunday – and the tune changed.

"Not only had he lied to me," Greenwell said, "he came in with a record year."

Each department has its own fund-raising techniques, he said. Edgewood would hold a street festival with booths, as would Camp Taylor. McMahan will hit the Crusade hard beginning two weeks before the deadline.

"It's strictly an effort of love," he said. "The only thing the departments really compete against is last year's numbers. The worst thing a department can go through is to come in, go on stage and say, 'We're down from last year.' That's just something no chief wants to do."

Members of Dixie Suburban Fire Department head out to collect at Crusade roadblocks on the always busy Dixie Highway.

New Haven, Ky. Firefighters gather around the station before heading out to raise money for the Crusade.

Chief Robert Gaddie of Jeffersontown Fire Department sits with fire coordinator Gary Doyle

Greenwell said he has been to national conferences with other firefighters, and has tried to explain the power and endurance of the Crusade to them, but "they just can't fathom it."

He told a story of working a road block at Outer Loop and Old Shepherdsville Road, in pouring rain. On Crusade weekend, many drivers keep a cup filled with coins on the seat next to them, ready for the next road block at the next intersection.

"This one particular case, a man probably in his 80s," Greenwell said, "he had a handful of change. We were standing out in the driving rain and I walked up to him with a boot, hat or whatever and he put his container on the seat, reached in his wallet, holding up traffic, and he got out a handful of bills.

"He said, 'If you're willing to stand out in this kind of heat and rain, you're worth more than change.'"

As with many firefighters, Greenwell also had a deeply personal story explaining his drive to be a part of 30 Crusades.

"The first three years I had been involved with the fire department collecting and road blocking, I had already instilled in my mind, 'We're out doing this for other people. That's why we're here.'

"Suddenly I got a call that my daughter had delivered premature twins at St. Anthony's Hospital. They were 26 weeks. One was a pound and three ounces and the other was a pound and six ounces.

"They transferred them immediately to Children's Hospital by way of a baby buggy – a special pediatric ambulance or premature ambulance they had there.

"Well, when we got down there the next day the twins, of course, were under treatment in the little perambulators and all the machinery. We would look around, and most of the equipment in there, including the perambulator they were in, had a chrome tag on it saying, 'A gift from the Crusade for Children.'" The twins would grow up to be healthy, happy adults. Bill Greenwell was changed forever.

"All of a sudden I wasn't doing it for anyone else anymore. I had gotten the benefits of it myself. And there's probably not a department involved that hasn't been touched by the Crusade in one way or another."

Although the larger fire departments often got the most publicity, by the mid-1970s well over 100 departments were collecting money in the widening Crusade net – including Russell Springs, Columbia/Adair, Lancaster, Sonora, Leitchfield and Lebanon in Kentucky, and Austin, Milltown, Crothersville, Utica, Palmyra, Scottsburg and Salem in Indiana.

It was, in fact, the nearly $11,000 contribution from the Lake Dreamland Fire Department in 1977 that gave the Crusade its first $1,000,000 total in its 24-year history.

And the Crusade had been ready for it. Executive director Phyllis Knight had asked that an extra window be added to the Crusade tote board to accommodate the seventh digit. Pleasure Ridge Park firefighter Ron Leatherman held up seven-year-old cerebral palsy patient Shannon Gaston alongside the board.

Then, as the Crusade band played "The Impossible Dream" and balloons cascaded from the ceiling, Shannon opened the new tote board window and flipped the "one million dollar" switch.

The tons of change brought in sometimes get a little too heavy and land on the floor.

Never fear, there are dozens of volunteers on hand to ensure that every piece of change is found and put back into the fishbowls.

Employees of Standard Gravure took on the assignment of carrying the fish bowls of money during Crusade weekend. These volunteers are working hard to receive the Crusade Hernia Award, which is given to money carriers each year.

"I love it," Shannon's mother, Joyce Gaston, told The Courier-Journal. "I guess when you have a child like this, you see the Crusade work."

That million-dollar effort was aided by Louisville native and singer Helen Humes – who donated $200 of her check to the Crusade. Singing star Jim Stafford stayed on stage until about 3 a.m. that Sunday, went back to his hotel and heard WHAS radio star Wayne Perkey say nice things about him, then returned to the studio.

"I'm tired, but I'm wired into this thing," he explained.

By then the Crusade was spreading its money among 90 agencies to help children. The "Moral Side of the News" panel included Dr. Donald Burke of Highland Baptist Church, Monsignor Alfred Horrigan of St. James Catholic Church, Dr. Herbert Waller of Adath Israel Temple, Dr. Jo Riley of the First Christian Church and Rev. Lincoln Bingham of the West End Baptist Church.

A year later the Crusade collected $1,243,500.74 to celebrate its 25th anniversary. Along with the perpetual high level "local" talent offered by Jo Ann Hale, Judy Marshall, Dean Shepherd, Pee Wee King and the Patsy Bloor dancers, the "national" talent pool was filled with Diahann Carroll, Donald O'Connor (who by all accounts also took a strong liking to Kentucky's distilled spirits) and Vic Tayback, the gruff, hard-nosed "Mel" in the hit TV show "Alice."

Tayback, a gregarious and likeable man, spent some of the night visiting local watering holes with Crusade staff members, among them the S&H Lounge up the street from WHAS.

According to longtime Crusade money-carrier Bob Smith, who was with the group, two fairly inebriated S&H regulars kept staring at Tayback, thinking he looked familiar, but unable to figure out who he was.

The ever-helpful S&H management took Tayback into the kitchen, gave him an apron and chef's hat to wear, and sent him back out to the drunks for closer inspection. They still couldn't figure out who he was.

The Crusade hit the jackpot in recognizable stars in 1979 with the appearance of Bobby Rydell, Della Reese, Tim Reid, Arnie Lawrence and last, but certainly not least in the kiddies' eyes, Bob Keeshan – "Captain Kangaroo."

Continuing a fun Crusade tradition, Rydell stuck around to the end, hitched a ride on a fire truck and visited a neighborhood bar to collect.

Jim Walton retired from his Crusade emcee work in 1979 after 26 years at the microphone – to be replaced by Wayne Perkey. Hundreds of volunteers gave Walton a minute-long standing ovation.

That also was the year the Okolona and Pleasure Ridge Park firefighters took their friendly feud a little farther when Okolona firefighters removed an American flag from a PRP firehouse and the car keys from the auto of PRP chief R. K. Back.

So a PRP firefighter wrote a poem that said:

You can take my flag
You can take my keys
But we're still No. 1
In the big mo-NEY.

Bobby Rydell appeared on the Crusade telethon in 1977 and 1979.

Actress Diahann Carroll performs on the 1978 Crusade.

"Captain Kangaroo" (Bob Keeshan) participated in several Crusades over the years.

The
Twenty-Fifth
WHAS
Crusade for
Children

Crusade 25

As the Crusade moved into 1980, it was finally incorporated as a nonprofit organization — and received its largest single gift up to that time, an $80,284 bequest from the will of Catherine O. Bishop. On another level of donations, the Eminence Fire Department brought in $3,694 in cash and coins stuffed into a 10-foot section of fire hose.

The Archdiocese of Louisville brought in $72,250, pushing its total Crusade contributions past $1 million. Louisville humorist Grady Nutt — who would be killed two years later in a plane crash — was one of the stars of that show.

It ended more than 24 hours after it started — a record length at that time — with Perkey holding eight-year-old cerebral palsy patient Sandy Kays as hundreds of volunteers, with tears in many eyes, joined him on stage to sing "God Bless America."

In 1981 Phyllis Knight resigned as Crusade director, being replaced by WHAS veteran Bud Harbsmeier. By then the more than 120 volunteer fire departments were reaching out in an almost 100-mile-wide circle around Louisville — a band of love and caring. The Crusade raised $1,584,307.96 that year — with expenses of only $68,125.24, or 4.3 percent.

Carefully recorded in the Crusade notebook was the fact that guest star Marilyn Michaels had become difficult to deal with, said she was sick and needed chicken soup, and WHAS president Bob Morse had to find it. The ever-expanding Crusade also lasted 24 hours and 55 minutes that year.

As the Crusade hit its 30th year in 1983, its president was Morse; the executive director was Harbsmeier, the producer was George Hulcher, the director Dave Jones and the emcee was Perkey.

The absolute highlight of the talent show that year — or perhaps any of the first 30 years — was Courier-Journal publisher Barry Bingham Jr., a classical-music aficionado, singing with the country-fried Hager Twins.

Other local talent that year again included Jo Ann Hale and Judy Marshall, a pair given a deserved tribute by Louisville Times television critic Vince Staten. Marshall said she had made her first appearance in 1954 as a high school sophomore, and Hale had begun in 1961 after being hired as a staff vocalist at WHAS.

Marshall told Staten about one of her special memories of the Crusade: "Jim Walton took me to the hotel and told me there was somebody there he wanted me to meet. It turned out to be Zippy the chimpanzee."

Marshall said she walked Zippy back to the Crusade, and what began as a joke turned into a wonderful moment:

"The monkey was sitting in my lap. And there was this little blind boy there and he was asking me questions about Zippy and then he would reach up and touch him. And Zippy just sat there and let him. It was very touching to me."

At age 30, the Crusade had raised almost $18 million for special-needs children, with more than 130 fire departments and hundreds of other groups and organizations contributing.

The Courier-Journal and Louisville Times showcased many stories that year about children — and families — who had received help.

One child was 12-year-old Steven Coots, the son of Danny and Bonita Coots of Pleasure Ridge Park. While Steven mowed the lawn, a nail shot into his chest.

Crusade emcees Wayne Perkey and Jim Walton pose together during Crusade weekend in 1980.

Crusade pioneers (l-r) Phyllis Knight and Jim Walton are honored for their hard work and dedication to helping Kentuckiana's special needs children by Bobby Rydell and Wayne Perkey.

A preliminary X-ray did not show the full damage. Steven was referred to Kosair Children's Hospital, where surgeons used a special heart-and-lung machine – purchased in part with a $40,944 gift from the Crusade – to remove a bent nail from the right ventricle of his heart.

"That morning," Bonita Coots said, "we realized what the Crusade really means. It's wonderful."

Debbe Sublett, a mother of three, told the story of the Crusade for Children Charity Ball, which she and her husband, Jim, a pediatric allergist, had begun as a fund-raiser with about 25 of their friends.

She said her brother had received his first hearing aid from the Crusade, and the Crusade had helped her sister with a leg problem – a sister who went on to become a scholarship basketball player.

The birth of her third child had been complicated by Sublett's benign brain tumor, but when the child was born healthy it made her realize all the more how lucky she had been – and she wanted others to have healthy children, too.

"That's what the Crusade is all about," she said.

Then 12-year-old Sean Kerberg of Louisville was born with brain damage, and doctors feared he might be blind. He was placed on life support funded by the Crusade at Kosair Children's Hospital. Years later, the Crusade supplied visual aid that helped him read and get through school.

"Oh, my goodness," said his grandmother, Viola McCoy of Valley Station. "If we hadn't had that help I don't know what would have happened. I guess he would have sat in a corner all his life."

The Kentucky Advocate in Danville printed a story about the growing influence of the Crusade in the more rural areas of the state. It said Boyle, Mercer and Garrard counties had each been participating in the Crusade.

The return of the Crusade money to those counties enabled the Boyle County school system to begin a program for mentally handicapped children. A $6,500 grant to the Danville Early Learning Center went toward purchasing a car to transport children to and from school. A $4,500 grant to the Lexington Early Learning Center helped it begin operations.

For its 30th birthday, the Crusade also honored the 15 people who had been with it since 1954. They included Joe and Henrietta Laffoon, Carmel Cullen, Jack Koch, Sam Gifford, Bob Pilkington, Dick Sweeney, Dave Dumeyer, Jim Topmiller, Dave Jones, Milton Metz, John McCrory, Clarence Hash, Ted Throckmorton and Omer Tucker.

WHAS Crusade for Children
30
1954
1983

Celebrities, volunteers, and WHAS staff celebrate 25 years of helping Kentucky and Indiana's special needs children

Moving into its fourth decade in the mid-1980s, the ever-growing Crusade continually had to adapt to growth – and losses.

The upside was obvious: With singer John Davidson and Elvis impersonator Eddie Miles doing the heavy entertainment lifting, the 1985 Crusade brought in $2,085,431.27 – the first to break the $2 million barrier.

Clearly Elvis's presence, at least, was still in the building. In an odd footnote, however, the pleasant, mild-mannered Davidson became the object of the Crusade's only "death threat" – and required round-the-clock protection.

On stage, Davidson and Miles were joined by the usual cast of giving characters – local favorites Jo Ann Hale, Karen Kraft, Judy Marshall, Dean Shepherd, Dr. Tim Stivers and Ange Humphrey, along with almost 200 fire departments from more than 40 counties in Kentucky and Southern Indiana.

But money also poured into the firefighters' boots from recycling centers collecting old newspapers and cans, a Crusade Night at the Louisville Redbirds game and special collections at General Electric. Louisville resident Peggy J. Smith left $207,000 to the Crusade in a will – then the largest single donation ever.

Jeffersonville's Robert Hedge, owner of the legendary Bob's Pub near the Ohio River, continually added to the money flow by confiscating every loose nickel in the bar for the children, and then staging a "Stick Horse Derby" with each child entered given jockey's silks, a cap and a stick horse to race.

"As far as I know," said Crusade director Bud Harbsmeier, perhaps stating the obvious, "this is the only Stick Horse Derby in Southern Indiana."

Another big push came from the Milton, Ky. Volunteer Fire Department. According to a memo sent to WHAS and WAMZ-FM air staffs by executive Brench Boden, the Milton firefighters were holding the most gigantic celebrity auction in local history, including a pair of white jeans (size 29) once wrapped around actress Dyan Cannon, and a Jack Klugman recipe for spaghetti.

Then there was this memo sent to Jefferson County police officer Bob Yates, confirming yet another interesting fund-raising adventure on the way to $2 million.

Dear Officer Yates:

This is to confirm receipt of $11,901.90 in cash for the WHAS Crusade for Children. The money had been confiscated by Jefferson County Police in a gambling raid 12 months ago, and recently ordered released to the Crusade by Circuit Judge Ellen Ewing.
Please thank all members of the County Police team who aided in this seizure. Thanks too for escorting the cash and me to Citizens Fidelity bank. Enclosed is a copy of the bank's receipt.

Sincerely
Bud Harbsmeier

Continually seeking ways to extend its reach and yet simultaneously reduce air time – which was pushing an insomniac 28 hours – the 1985 Crusade for the

5

A DREAM
FULFILLED -
THE
CRUSADE
AT FORTY

Local performer Judy Marshall has been a Crusade favorite for many years.

JoAnne Hale was the second part of the Dynamic Duo that included Judy Marshall.

Harrods Creek Fire Department poses for a picture with WHAS-TV meteorologist Chuck Taylor (front row, second from right).

first time used a helicopter to visit three local counties, videotape the giving, and keep the fire trucks closer to home.

The mid-1980s also reflected the growing number of agencies receiving money from the Crusade. The Crusade panel of Dr. Larry Dipboye of Buechel Park Baptist Church, Msgr. Alfred Horrigan of St. James, Dr. Herbert Waller of The Temple, Dr. William Slider of Christ United Methodist Church and Dr. Donald Cockerham of Zion Baptist Church made 147 grants to 29 Kentucky and 10 Indiana counties in 1984 – with all money collected in each state returned to that state.

The grants were widespread, including

- $396,000 to Kosair Children's Hospital
- $36,000 to the Adair County Board of Education for a classroom for trainable mentally-handicapped students
- $36,000 to Clark County's New Hope Services for a bus and van
- $22,000 to Taylor County for computers and a bus.

The biggest change in 1985 was the decision by Harbsmeier and WHAS executive Bob Morse to move Crusade weekend from May to early June. Not only was May a ratings period, but TV and radio staffs also were very busy with the Kentucky Derby each May, and there was often a primary election.

The saddest news of 1985 was the death of Jim Walton, the man called "Mr. Crusade." He had emceed 26 Crusades, then stuck around to help in more. To honor Walton, Harbsmeier and others inaugurated a Jim Walton Memorial Trophy to be given annually to the two fire departments with the largest percentage increase of funds. With ever-increasing fund-raising, the trophies now go to four departments.

Before being named Crusade director in 1982, Harbsmeier had worked for WHAS-TV as a reporter for 20 years. That job that had given him insight into the wonder of the event, but very little information about all its moving parts. "In those first years, like everybody else I had an assignment to be at a certain place at a certain time," he said. "The first thing I remember doing was helping to lug the money off the stage at Memorial Auditorium.

"You might remember a picture of people in the money room handing sacks of money through a window to somebody with an armored car. But I had absolutely no idea what all was involved."

Harbsmeier said he had about eight months to get ready for his first Crusade – and previous director Phyllis Knight for a brief time, to fill him in on the details. "In 1982 it was a Lone Ranger operation," he said, "and I had Phyllis with me maybe two weeks trying to tell me what was involved.

"I had a little office – she had a little office - right off Sixth Street and it was crammed with file cabinets. Everything at that time was done by pen or pencil, and after two weeks I was the only guy doing it. It was just incredible to think of everything that was involved."

Harbsmeier's first goal became to establish personal contact with each

WHAS Radio's Milton Metz (third from left) and WHAS-TV Anchor Jim Mitchell (to Metz's right) seen here interviewing the Crusade Panel of Ministers.

Jim "Mr. Crusade" Walton seen here signing autographs for children.

Bud Harbsmeier (c) poses with singer Terry Gibbs (r) and her road manager(l) after Terry's performance in 1985.

of the volunteer fire departments, which were bringing in more than 50 percent of the Crusade money.

"Usually the department would invite me for a chicken dinner, or something," he said. "My wife went with me, because the Crusade is very much family oriented and we'd sit around and talk about the problems parents face." Harbsmeier's second task was to try to add a computer to the operation – a piece of equipment then fairly rare at WHAS.

"I knew we needed something like that so when somebody from a fire department called and asked, 'How much money did we raise in 1976?' I could tell them.

"Down through the years I was able to enlist the aid of a number of computer experts from around the city who would volunteer their time to come up with computer programs that were directly related to the Crusade, something for the fire departments, for letter writing, for record keeping.

"The money that was saved was incredible. At Crusade time, the lobby was filled with computers and people working computers, all donated by various companies."

Over his almost 20 years as director, Harbsmeier also saw local companies and agencies become more involved. They included Kroger – which became a huge supporter – Norton Healthcare, Jefferson County Schools, Louisville Gas & Electric, WHAS employees, Dairy Queen restaurants, General Electric and professional golfer Fuzzy Zoeller, whose Wolf Creek Challenge held at his Covered Bridge Golf Course near Sellersburg, Ind., would raise hundreds of thousands of dollars.

National City Bank also became a huge supporter of the Crusade, not only in supplying almost 200 volunteers each year to process all the money and checks, but also in waiving any investment fees and providing investment advice. "They would sit in one of the rooms and process everything," Harbsmeier said. "Every bit of the money that came into the Crusade was in the bank Monday morning."

Jefferson County Public School employees and students make their proud contribution to the Crusade early Sunday morning.

Fairdale Fire Department makes its donation during Crusade 31 in 1984.

The benchmark years for Harbsmeier were those when the Crusade passed the next million-dollar mark, each one seeming almost impossible to reach – then becoming commonplace.

"The community wasn't really growing that much, populationwise," he said. "But yet the same people continued to give more and more every year. It was just an amazing thing to see."

Harbsmeier retired on Dec. 31, 2000. Along with the direct satisfaction that comes with helping to save lives, Harbsmeier said what he misses most about being director is the relationship with the thousands of people who were involved. "People that I only saw maybe once or twice a year and I considered them to be very good friends," he said. "I had a real feeling I had accomplished something, better than I ever had as a reporter.

"Each Crusade... knowing that it was going to save a lot of lives and make a big, big difference, and I was a part of that, and I feel good about that."

In 1986 the Crusade faced the biggest potential problem it could ever have: the breakup and sale of the Bingham family empire, including the three prime contributors to the Crusade: WHAS-TV, WHAS-AM radio and WAMZ-FM radio.

In addition, the family newspapers, The Courier-Journal and the Louisville Times, and its Standard Gravure printing company had made enormous contributions in time, money and volunteer workers.

Robert Morse, president of WHAS Inc., sounded an optimistic note about the impending sale in a Courier-Journal interview:

"I expect the last thing in the world they (the new owners) would want to do is mess with that," Morse said of the Crusade. "It's not only a sacred cow at WHAS, it's a sacred cow within the community."

The 1986 Crusade – held on the rainy, hot and humid weekend of June 7th and 8th – raised $2,440,507.50, another record. In addition, the Providence Journal Co., the new owners of WHAS-TV, pledged to continue the Crusade for at least five years – and company vice president Jack Clifford came to Louisville to watch most of the show.

"My company is committed to maintaining the Crusade for as long as we own the stations," Clifford would say in a Courier-Journal interview. Clear Channel Communications, the new owner of the Bingham radio stations, also pledged continuing support of the Crusade.

"Seeing all those firemen bring in money to help children really turns me on," said Lowry Mayes, president of Clear Channel.

The 1986 Crusade used a new set donated by Levy's Building and Supply and designed by Harry Campbell – the first new model in decades.

A remote Crusade stage was used for the first time, allowing singer Billy Joe Royal to entertain a live audience in Pleasure Ridge Park. Which turned out to be the best place to be, as the air conditioning failed inside a hot and steamy WHAS-TV studio, invoking memories of the good old days at Memorial Auditorium. A high point of the evening was the Black Mudd Volunteer Fire Department's bringing a huge, pizza-sized cookie with its logo on it – along with $22,463.93.

Harbsmeier also received a note from Barry Bingham, Sr, the man whose vision had helped start the Crusade 33 years earlier. The note came in response to a Harbsmeier invitation to Bingham to come to the studio for the final Bingham-era Crusade – which had then raised $26,904,338.99 for children in need.

Milton Metz (c) speaks with The Crusade Saturday night show audience.

Bud Harbsmeier and Wayne Perkey host a Crusade radio show on 84WHAS with one of the Hager Twins.

This little boy is getting his blood pressure checked by equipment purchased with a Crusade grant for the Children and Youth Project at the University of Louisville.

Bud,

Thanks for your invitation. I'd like to be there, but I'm afraid it would be an event of pretty heavy emotional stress for my wife and me.
I think we will watch it on TV this time.

BB

The 1987 Crusade, which took in $2,300,082.52, was only the second to fall short of the previous year's amount, but it was close, times were tight, and the $200,000 received in wills that year was less than before – but an area of donations very hard to predict.

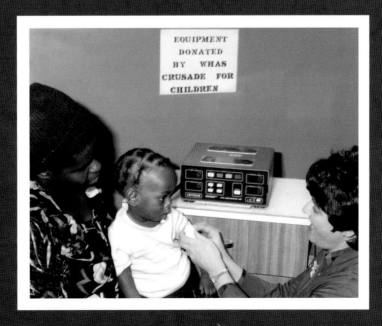

EQUIPMENT
DONATED
BY WHAS
CRUSADE FOR
CHILDREN

But the production news continued to be good. The use of a new satellite uplink truck and the helicopter allowed 50 volunteer fire departments that had been driving to Louisville to stay closer to home. The U. S. Army at Fort Knox added a production truck, allowing a live stage in the Hikes Point area.

Local bowlers continued to be involved, with the 18th annual Bowl for the Crusade at Thelmal Lanes and J-Town Lanes bringing in amateur and pro keglers Mike Aulby, Mark Roth, Bob Handley, Joe Berardi and Steve Martin for a season-long program that raised about $15,000 a year for kids.

As more encouragement of its willingness to be part of the Crusade, the Providence Journal Co., with Jack Clifford in Louisville, gave $70,000. Clear Channel, with Lowry Mayes in attendance, gave $5,000, and employees of The Courier-Journal, now owned by Gannett, Inc., donated $10,900. WHAS president Bob Morse resigned that year, replaced by Neil Kuvin, whose first week in town included the Crusade.

Crusade weekend – which actually might include a month of weekends for some volunteers collecting at intersections – could be annoying to some motorists getting tired of seeing someone with a hand, or boot, out at seemingly every light and stop sign.

It was a complaint forever answered in 1987 in a letter-to-the-editor signed by Dick Sanders of Louisville – part of which is quoted below:

"I hope you will print this confession – and apology – to the woman who wrote complaining of being badgered by volunteer firefighters during the WHAS Crusade for Children. You see, I am that firefighter who asked her to give just one more time.

Yes, ma'am, I know you had already given at other intersections…Yes, I even came to your home; and if you work in my district, you probably saw me at your place of employment as well. I think I also went to your church.

I don't know why I do it. It's like a sickness I have once a year, every year, for the last 34 years. Maybe it's because I know that premature babies weighing only 2 pounds now have a 72 percent chance of survival in our community thanks to the Crusade for Children. Or maybe it's because I know the Home of the Innocents needs a quarter million dollar addition.

There is no cure for my illness, but I can suggest something that might make you feel better. Next year, as the first week of June approaches, decide how much you would like to give at all intersections combined.

Then, next time you are at the bank, convert this amount to coins. Keep these coins in your automobile during the Crusade. Then, each time a boot is offered to you at an intersection, drop in one or two coins.

You might even say something like, 'Keep up the good work, fellas' or 'How are we doing this year?' All you will get in return is a sweaty smile and a hoarse 'Thank You.'"

The 1988 Crusade raised $2,504,878.94, with the Rough River and Edgewood fire departments winning the Walton Trophies. In spite of technological improvements, the show lasted until 3:15 Monday morning, with about a dozen

WHAS-TV Facilities Manager (r) Jerry Gliessner and others take a break in the Crusade action.

Wives of U.S. Military fighting in the 1991 Gulf War collected money for the Crusade.

Students at Bellarmine University's Learning Center are assisted by Crusade grants.

people left in the studio, a few of them probably too sleepy to speak. Two months after that Crusade, founder Barry Bingham Sr., died at age 82.

In 1989 the Crusade moved its act – and acts – to the Bomhard Theater at the Kentucky Center for the Arts, with country singer Gary Morris and Louisvillian and gospel singer Larnell Harris as featured acts.

The move proved prosperous, as the Crusade broke another million-dollar barrier, pulling in $3,037,400.86 – including $431,805.99 in wills. That included the then-largest will in history, $253,534.66 from Vera Stober of Louisville, and $139,279.11 from Belle Wheeler of Floyd County, Ind.

As a sign of the economic times, the new station owners instructed the Crusade to pay all bills itself; most of them had been paid by the Bingham companies in previous years.

The Crusade moved into 1990 with another loss, the death of Vic Sholis, so the 37th Crusade was dedicated in his honor.

A special hit that year was blind fiddler Michael Cleveland of Southern Indiana. The little boy would grow up to be named Bluegrass Fiddler of the Year twice in national polls.

The entertainment headliner was B. J. Thomas, whose hit "Raindrops Keep Fallin' on My Head" seemed way too prophetic as a fierce band of tornadoes again fired up during Crusade weekend – this time sending all performers, volunteers, technicians and the audience into the basement parking garage of the Kentucky Center for the Arts as funnels touched down in Clark and Floyd counties in Indiana.

Long-time Crusade emcee and WHAS radio host Wayne Perkey has vivid memories of that early June night:

"The Kentucky Center for the Arts welcomed us, and the irony was B. J. Thomas had just begun his song when there was this sudden clap of thunder, and we cut away to meteorologist Ken Schulz, who was at the TV station, and he said, 'Wayne, there is a tornado watch out and we're going to have to take it away.'

"So for the next, I guess hour or so, it was Ken Schulz interrupting what was going on in the Bomhard Theater and doing an update on the weather. "And about 10:30 or 11 p.m. the lady who was in charge of the theater at the time walked on stage and right in front of me – and I'm doing whatever I'm doing – and said, 'Everybody in the basement, right now!'

"And I said, 'But wait, we're live.' She said, 'Never mind that, everybody in the basement, now!' So we all went downstairs and spent the next three or four hours waiting out the tornado alert. B. J. Thomas hasn't been back, I don't think."

Perkey had come to WHAS from Alabama in 1969, in part because of a story he'd read about the Crusade in a trade publication. He would become only its second emcee – following the legendary Jim Walton – and also had vivid memories of his first show as host:

"Was I scared the first night? Absolutely. I didn't know it but I was scared to death. I spent most of the last part of the rehearsal time running back and forth to the bathroom.

"I am such an emotional guy, such a sentimental guy that what I was really

"Hee-Haw" performers the Hager Twins were WHAS employee favorites during their Crusade performance.

Crusade MC Wayne Perkey interviews Miss Kentucky Kelly Lin Brumagen.

These children enjoy the music of the Crusade as they dance the night away at the Kentucky Center.

afraid of was the show would open, the band would play, the singers would sing, the kids would dance and then the spotlight would come down and here would be that one little child walking through the spotlight up to the host.

"And I thought, you know, I'm going to reach down and pick him up and all that emotion is going to be filling the auditorium and I'm gonna just well up with tears and I won't even be able to say, 'Here we are.'

"I thought, 'How am I going to handle that? I'll burst into tears, I won't be able to carry on, the whole thing will die and it will be my fault.'"

Perkey said what saved him was that a boy with spina bifida came hobbling across the stage, reached up and grabbed Perkey's nose – cutting it a little with his fingernails.

That was a reality check, bringing Perkey back down to earth – but also requiring frequent dabbing at his nose to stop the bleeding during a live broadcast. Basketball bounced onto the Crusade stage in 1990 with a special game between the 1980 and 1986 University of Louisville NCAA basketball champions, a showdown in which Louisville legend Darrell Griffith and his 1980 buddies Jerry Eaves, Wiley Brown and Rodney and Scooter McCray met Pervis Ellison and Billy Thompson of the 1986 champs before 14,971 fans in Freedom Hall. The 1980 team won 101-96, but the larger winners were the Crusade – and Kentucky Harvest – which took home about $40,000 each.

Overall the Crusade took in $2,807,948.09 in 1990, down a little from the year before but still remarkable considering so many of the fire departments and emergency units were mixing time between tornado duty and raising money for children.

The Crusade ended 40 years of service by reaching into almost all 120 Kentucky counties and an ever-widening area of Southern Indiana. That 40th show featured The Captain and Tennille on June 5, 1993, for its Bomhard Theater show – with Roger Dane then conducting the Crusade Orchestra.

It would raise an incredible $4.5 million, a great deal of that due to the surprise generosity of one man, a Meade County farmer named Johnny Pack, who left more than $700,000 to the Crusade.

Pack, who died at 83, was described as an old-fashioned, close-mouthed farmer who did his banking in bib overalls, yet told his lawyer in 1984 he wanted to leave most of his estate – including a 231-acre farm – to the Crusade because he thought it was a good charity and he wanted to help children.

Yet no one had ever heard Pack, a bachelor, mention the Crusade. Nor had he been known to donate money to the Meade County firemen who came to his modest farmhouse during Crusade drives.

Pack also left $40,000 each to his 12 nieces and nephews. One of them, Doris Keys, told Courier-Journal columnist Byron Crawford:

"We didn't have any idea he had that much money. Of course we knew the farm was valuable, but the way he lived you'd think he didn't have a penny to his name."

Other estates left to the Crusade that year meant it had more than $1 million in the bank before any other fund-raising had begun. The Archdiocese of Louisville, General Electric and Alliant Health Service employees were generous. For the first time the Kentucky Corrections Department, including all state reformatories, contributed money.

WHAS CRUSADE 36 FOR CHILDREN

WHAS-TV's Dave Conrad (l) interviews University of Louisville Basketball Star Darrell "Dr. Dunkenstein" Griffith and 84WHAS radio's Gary Burbank.

(l-r) Bud Harbsmeier, Father B.J. Breen, Archbishop Thomas Kelly, Wayne Perkey during the 1992 Crusade.

Money Carriers entertain themselves on the side of the set as they wait for the next group of fishbowls.

The Crusade had more than come full circle in its 40 years. That was evident in a 1992 Courier-Journal story about Hanna Miller, the granddaughter of Barry Bingham Sr. She had been born three months premature – 12 inches long and weighing only 1 pound 12 ounces.

Hanna spent her first three months at Kosair Children's Hospital, much of it in the neonatal intensive-care unit, where almost every piece of equipment bore the words "Crusade for Children."

Barry Bingham, Sr. never saw Hanna, said her mother, Eleanor Bingham Miller, but one reason he helped start the Crusade was to help children like her. In the early 1990s residents and agencies in the ever-widening areas served by the Crusade continued to find ingenious and creative ways to raise money.

New Albany VFW Post 1693 raffled a new pickup truck. The Kroger Co. became heavily involved, with one store manager, Randy Nesbit, suffering the indignity of a shaved head after employees met a $12,000 store challenge.

The Louisville Radio Control Club raised money at a model airplane display. Kern's Kitchens baked a 500-pound Derby pie. Students at Coleridge-Taylor Elementary School built shoebox floats. The Manzanita Tribe No. 276 – which traditionally closed the show each year – held a dance. The Lake Dreamland Fire Department held a "Putting On the Hits" lip-sync show.

The expanding Walton Trophy winners in 1993 were the Annetta Volunteer Fire Department in Grayson County, the Shepherdsville Fire Department and McMahan Fire Department – for the third time in four years.

In its 40 years the Crusade had raised almost $50 million, was contributing to more than 200 agencies, and had touched the lives of millions of people – parents and children.

Its grants were going to Lone Jack Elementary School in the mountains of Eastern Kentucky, the Special Olympics in Casey County, the Bluegrass Technical Center in Fayette County, and the Cerebral Palsy School in Louisville. Money was sent to the Cumberland River Mental Health Organization in Laurel County, Western Kentucky University in Warren County, and the Ohio County Board of Education.

In Indiana, grants were being sent to Clark, Floyd, Harrison, Jackson, and Orange and Switzerland counties – with the best yet to come.

Crusade Executive Director Dan Miller thanks the thousands of Crusaders from across Kentucky and Indiana for their dedication to changing children's lives at the 50th Anniversary Reunion.

Emily Stilwell of the Miracle Dancers is able to perform thanks to the generous donations made to the WHAS Crusade for Children.

A smiling girl shows the spirit of the Crusade for the next generation.

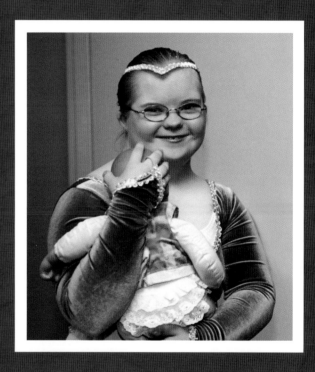

FIRE DEPARTMENTS THAT HAVE CONTRIBUTED TO
THE WHAS CRUSADE FOR CHILDREN
DURING THE FIRST 50 YEARS

KENTUCKY DEPARTMENTS	COUNTY
ANCHORAGE VOLUNTEER FIRE DEPARTMENT & EMS	JEFFERSON
ANDERSON COUNTY FIRE PROTECTION DISTRICT	ANDERSON
ANNETA VOLUNTEER FIRE DEPARTMENT	GRAYSON
BAGDAD FIRE PROTECTION DISTRICT	SHELBY
BALLARDSVILLE RURAL FIRE DEPARTMENT	OLDHAM
BARDSTOWN - NELSON COUNTY FIRE DEPARTMENT	NELSON
BARREN COUNTY FIREFIGHTERS ASSOCIATION	BARREN
BATTLETOWN VOLUNTEER FIRE DEPARTMENT	MEADE
BEDFORD VOLUNTEER FIRE DEPARTMENT	TRIMBLE
BELL COUNTY FIRE DEPARTMENTS	BELL
BELL COUNTY FORESTRY CAMP	BELL
BLACK MUDD FIRE DISTRICT	JEFFERSON
BLOOMFIELD FIRE DEPARTMENT	NELSON
BONNIEVILLE VOLUNTEER FIRE DEPARTMENT	HART
BOSTON VOLUNTEER FIRE DEPARTMENT	NELSON
BOYLE COUNTY FIRE DEPARTMENTS	BOYLE
BRADFORDSVILLE VOLUNTEER FIRE DEPARTMENT	MARION
BREEDING VOLUNTEER FIRE DEPARTMENT	ADAIR
BUECHEL FIRE DISTICT	JEFFERSON
BUFFALO VOLUNTEER FIRE DEPARTMENT	LARUE
BURGIN VOLUNTEER FIRE DEPARTMENT	MERCER
CAMP DICK VOLUNTEER FIRE DEPARTMENT	GARRARD
CAMP TAYLOR FIRE DISTRICT	JEFFERSON
CAMPBELLSBURG VOLUNTEER FIRE DEPARTMENT	HENRY
CAMPBELLSVILLE - TAYLOR COUNTY VOLUNTEER FIRE DEPARTMENT	TAYLOR
CANEYVILLE VOLUNTEER FIRE DEPARTMENT	GRAYSON
CARROLLTON FIRE DEPARTMENT	CARROLL
CARTERSVILLE VOLUNTEER FIRE DEPARTMENT	GARRARD
CENTRAL HARDIN COUNTY VOLUNTEER FIRE DEPARTMENT	HARDIN
CLARKSON FIRE & RESCUE	GRAYSON
CLINTON COUNTY EMS	CLINTON
CLOVERPORT CITY VOLUNTEER FIRE DEPARTMENT	BRECKINRIDGE
COLUMBIA- ADAIR COUNTY VOLUNTEER FIRE DEPARTMENT	ADAIR
CRAB ORCHARD VOLUNTEER FIRE DEPARTMENT	LINCOLN
CUB RUN VOLUNTEER FIRE DEPARTMENT	HART
CUMBERLAND RIVER VOLUNTEER FIRE DEPARTMENT	LETCHER
CUSTER AREA VOLUNTEER FIRE DEPARTMENT	BRECKINRIDGE
DANVILLE FIRE DEPARTMENT	BOYLE

DIXIE SUBURBAN FIRE DISTRICT	JEFFERSON
EAST 60 VOLUNTEER FIRE DEPARTMENT	SHELBY
EAST GRAYSON FIRE & RESCUE	GRAYSON
EAST WASHINGTON VOLUNTEER FIRE DEPARTMENT	WASHINGTON
EASTWOOD FIRE DISTRICT	JEFFERSON
EDGEWOOD FIRE DISTRICT	JEFFERSON
EKRON VOLUNTEER FIRE DEPARTMENT	MEADE
ELIZABETHTOWN FIRE DEPARTMENT	HARDIN
EMINENCE FIRE & RESCUE	HENRY
FAIRDALE FIRE DISTRICT	JEFFERSON
FALLS OF ROUGH VOLUNTEER FIRE DEPARTMENT	GRAYSON
FERN CREEK FIRE DEPARTMENT	JEFFERSON
FLAHERTY VOLUNTEER FIRE DEPARTMENT	MEADE
FORKLAND VOLUNTEER FIRE DEPARTMENT	BOYLE
FRAKES VOLUNTEER FIRE DEPARTMENT	BELL
FRANKFORT FIRE DEPARTMENT & EMS	FRANKLIN
FRANKLIN COUNTY VOLUNTEER FIRE DEPARTMENT	FRANKLIN
GARRARD COUNTY VOLUNTEER FIRE DEPARTMENT	GARRARD
GLENDALE FIRE DEPARTMENT	HARDIN
GRAVEL SWITCH FIRE DEPARTMENT	MARION
GREEN COUNTY VOLUNTEER FIRE DEPARTMENT	GREEN
GREENSBURG VOLUNTEER FIRE DEPARTMENT	GREEN
HARDINSBURG VOLUNTEER FIRE DEPARTMENT	BRECKINRIDGE
HARDYVILLE VOLUNTEER FIRE DEPARTMENT	HART
HARNED AREA VOLUNTEER FIRE DEPARTMENT	BRECKINRIDGE
HARRODS CREEK FIRE DISTRICT	JEFFERSON
HARRODSBURG VOLUNTEER FIRE DEPARTMENT	MERCER
HAWESVILLE FIRE DEPARTMENT	HANCOCK
HIGHVIEW FIRE DISTRICT	JEFFERSON
HODGENVILLE FIRE DEPARTMENT	LARUE
HORSE CAVE VOLUNTEER FIRE DEPARTMENT	HART
IRVINGTON VOLUNTEER FIRE DEPARTMENT	BRECKINRIDGE
JAMESTOWN VOLUNTEER FIRE DEPARTMENT	RUSSELL
JEFFERSONTOWN FIRE DISTRICT	JEFFERSON
KENTUCKY 86 VOLUNTEER FIRE DEPARTMENT	HARDIN
KENTUCKY RIVER FIRE DEPARTMENT	HENRY
KENTUCKY STATE REFORMATORY AMBULANCE	OLDHAM
KNIFLEY AREA VOLUNTEER FIRE DEPARTMENT	ADAIR
LAGRANGE FIRE & RESCUE	OLDHAM
LAKE DREAMLAND FIRE DISTRICT	JEFFERSON
LAKE JERICHO VOLUNTEER FIRE DEPARTMENT	HENRY
LANCASTER CITY FIRE DEPARTMENT	GARRARD
LARUE COUNTY FIRE & RESCUE	LARUE
LAWRENCEBURG FIRE DEPARTMENT	ANDERSON
LEBANON JUNCTION VOLUNTEER FIRE DEPARTMENT	BULLITT

LEBANON VOLUNTEER FIRE DEPARTMENT	MARION
LEITCHFIELD VOLUNTEER FIRE DEPARTMENT	GRAYSON
LIBERTY FIRE DEPARTMENT	CASEY
LINCOLN FIRE DISTRICT	LINCOLN
LINWOOD VOLUNTEER FIRE DEPARTMENT	HART
LORETTO VOLUNTEER FIRE DEPARTMENT	MARION
LOUISVILLE FIRE & RESCUE	JEFFERSON
LYNDON FIRE DISTRICT	JEFFERSON
MACKVILLE VOLUNTEER FIRE DEPARTMENT	WASHINGTON
MAGNOLIA VOLUNTEER FIRE DEPARTMENT	LARUE
MCDANIELS VOLUNTEER FIRE DEPARTMENT	BRECKINRIDGE
MCKINNEY FIRE & RESCUE	LINCOLN
MCMAHAN FIRE DISTRICT	JEFFERSON
MCQUADY VOLUNTEER FIRE DEPARTMENT	BRECKINRIDGE
MEADE COUNTY FIRE & RESCUE	MEADE
MERCER COUNTY CENTRAL	MERCER
MIDDLESBORO FIRE DEPARTMENT	BELL
MIDDLETOWN FIRE DISTRICT	JEFFERSON
MILTON VOLUNTEER FIRE DEPARTMENT	TRIMBLE
MONTGOMERY COUNTY VOLUNTEER FIRE DEPARTMENT	MONTGOMERY
MT. EDEN VOLUNTEER FIRE DEPARTMENT	SHELBY
MT. WASHINGTON VOLUNTEER FIRE DEPARTMENT	BULLITT
MULDRAUGH VOLUNTEER FIRE DEPARTMENT	MEADE
MUNFORDVILLE VOLUNTEER FIRE DEPARTMENT	HART
NEW CASTLE VOLUNTEER FIRE DEPARTMENT	
& EMERGENCY SQUAD	HENRY
NEW HAVEN VOLUNTEER FIRE DEPARTMENT	NELSON
NEW HOPE VOLUNTEER FIRE DEPARTMENT	NELSON
NEW LIBERTY VOLUNTEER FIRE DEPARTMENT	OWEN
NICHOLASVILLE FIRE DEPARTMENT	JESSAMINE
NICHOLS VOLUNTEER FIRE DEPARTMENT	BULLITT
NORTH METCALFE COUNTY VOLUNTEER FIRE DEPARTMENT	METCALFE
NORTH OLDHAM FIRE DEPARTMENT	OLDHAM
NORTH POINT TRAINING CENTER	BOYLE
NORTHEAST NELSON FIRE DEPARTMENT	NELSON
NOVEON - ZEON INDUSTRIAL FIRE BRIGADE	JEFFERSON
OKOLONA FIRE DISTRICT	JEFFERSON
OWEN COUNTY VOLUNTEER FIRE DEPARTMENT	OWEN
OWENTON VOLUNTEER FIRE DEPARTMENT	OWEN
PAINT LICK VOLUNTEER FIRE DEPARTMENT	GARRARD
PAYNEVILLE VOLUNTEER FIRE DEPARTMENT	MEADE
PERRYVILLE VOLUNTEER FIRE DEPARTMENT	BOYLE
PEWEE VALLEY FIRE PROTECTION DISTRICT	OLDHAM
PINEVILLE CITY FIRE DEPARTMENT	BELL
PLEASURE RIDGE PARK FIRE DISTRICT	JEFFERSON

PLEASUREVILLE VOLUNTEER FIRE DEPARTMENT	HENRY
RADCLIFF VOLUNTEER FIRE DEPARTMENT	HARDIN
RAYWICK FIRE DEPARTMENT	MARION
RINEYVILLE VOLUNTEER FIRE DEPARTMENT	HARDIN
ROLLING FORK VOLUNTEER FIRE DEPARTMENT	NELSON
RUSSELL SPRINGS VOLUNTEER FIRE DEPARTMENT	RUSSELL
SHELBY COUNTY VOLUNTEER FIRE DEPARTMENT	SHELBY
SHELBYVILLE FIRE DEPARTMENT	SHELBY
SHEPHERDSVILLE FIRE & RESCUE	BULLITT
SHIVELY FIRE DISTRICT	JEFFERSON
SIMPSONVILLE VOLUNTEER FIRE DEPARTMENT	SHELBY
SONORA VOLUNTEER FIRE DEPARTMENT	HARDIN
SOUTH DIXIE FIRE DISTRICT	JEFFERSON
SOUTH OLDHAM VOLUNTEER FIRE DEPARTMENT	OLDHAM
SOUTHEAST BULLITT FIRE & RESCUE	BULLITT
SPARTA FIRE DEPARTMENT	GALLATIN
SPRINGFIELD VOLUNTEER FIRE DEPARTMENT	WASHINGTON
ST. MATTHEWS FIRE DISTRICT	JEFFERSON
STANFORD VOLUNTEER FIRE DEPARTMENT	LINCOLN
STEPHENSBURG VOLUNTEER FIRE DEPARTMENT	HARDIN
STEPHENSPORT VOLUNTEER FIRE DEPARTMENT	BRECKINRIDGE
SUMMERSVILLE VOLUNTEER FIRE DEPARTMENT	GREEN
TAYLORSVILLE - SPENCER COUNTY VOLUNTEER FIRE DEPARTMENT	SPENCER
UPTON FIRE & RESCUE	HARDIN
VALLEY CREEK AREA VOLUNTEER FIRE DEPARTMENT	HARDIN
VERSAILLES VOLUNTEER FIRE DEPARTMENT	WOODFORD
VINE GROVE VOLUNTEER FIRE DEPARTMENT	HARDIN
WADDY VOLUNTEER FIRE DEPARTMENT	SHELBY
WASHINGTON COUNTY VOLUNTEER FIRE DEPARTMENT	WASHINGTON
WAX VOLUNTEER FIRE DEPARTMENT	GRAYSON
WAYNESBURG VOLUNTEER FIRE DEPARTMENT	LINCOLN
WEBSTER VOLUNTEER FIRE DEPARTMENT	BRECKINRIDGE
WEST 720 VOLUNTEER FIRE DEPARTMENT	GRAYSON
WEST 84 VOLUNTEER FIRE DEPARTMENT	HARDIN
WEST POINT VOLUNTEER FIRE DEPARTMENT	HARDIN
WESTPORT VOLUNTEER FIRE DEPARTMENT	OLDHAM
WESTSIDE VOLUNTEER FIRE DEPARTMENT	CARROLL
WHITE MILLS VOLUNTEER FIRE DEPARTMENT	HARDIN
WILLISBURG VOLUNTEER FIRE DEPARTMENT	WASHINGTON
WOLF CREEK FIRE DEPARTMENT & RESCUE UNIT	MEADE
WOODFORD COUNTY VOLUNTEER FIRE DEPARTMENT	WOODFORD
WORTHINGTON FIRE DISTRICT	JEFFERSON
ZONETON FIRE DEPARTMENT	BULLITT

INDIANA DEPARTMENTS	COUNTY
BLUE RIVER VOLUNTEER FIRE DEPARTMENT	WASHINGTON
BOONE TOWNSHIP VOLUNTEER FIRE DEPARTMENT	HARRISON
BORDEN - WOODTOWNSHIP VOLUNTEER FIRE DEPARTMENT	CLARK
BROWNSTOWN VOLUNTEER FIRE DEPARTMENT	JACKSON
CAMPBELLSBURG VOLUNTEER FIRE DEPARTMENT	WASHINGTON
CARR TOWNSHIP FIRE TERRITORY	JACKSON
CHARLESTOWN VOLUNTEER FIRE DEPARTMENT	CLARK
CLARKSVILLE FIRE DEPARTMENT	CLARK
CLIFTY FIRE COMPANY #6	JEFFERSON
CORTLAND VOLUNTEER FIRE DEPARTMENT	JACKSON
CROTHERSVILLE - VERNON TOWNSHIP VOLUNTEER FIRE DEPARTMENT	JACKSON
DEPUTY VOLUNTEER FIRE DEPARTMENT	JEFFERSON
ELIZABETH VOLUNTEER FIRE DEPARTMENT	HARRISON
FREDERICKSBURG VOLUNTEER FIRE DEPARTMENT	WASHINGTON
FRENCH LICK FIRE DEPARTMENT	ORANGE
GEORGETOWN TOWNSHIP VOLUNTEER FIRE DEPARTMENT	FLOYD
GIBSON TOWNSHIP - LITTLE YORK VOLUNTEER FIRE DEPARTMENT	WASHINGTON
GREENVILLE TOWNSHIP VOLUNTEER FIRE DEPARTMENT	FLOYD
HANOVER VOLUNTEER FIRE DEPARTMENT	JEFFERSON
HARRISON TOWNSHIP - CORYDON VOLUNTEER FIRE DEPARTMENT	HARRISON
HETH TOWNSHIP VOLUNTEER FIRE DEPARTMENT	HARRISON
JACKSON TOWNSHIP VOLUNTEER FIRE DEPARTMENT	WASHINGTON
JEFFERSON & CRAIG TOWNSHIPS FIRE DEPARTMENT	SWITZERLAND
JEFFERSON COUNTY FIRE DEPARTMENTS	JEFFERSON
JEFFERSONVILLE FIRE DEPARTMENT	CLARK
JENNINGS TOWNSHIP VOLUNTEER FIRE DEPARTMENT	SCOTT
JOHNSON TOWNSHIP VOLUNTEER FIRE DEPARTMENT	SCOTT
KENT VOLUNTEER FIRE DEPARTMENT	JEFFERSON
LAFAYETTE TOWNSHIP VOLUNTEER FIRE DEPARTMENT	FLOYD
LANESVILLE VOLUNTEER FIRE DEPARTMENT	HARRISON
LEAVENWORTH VOLUNTEER FIRE DEPARTMENT	CRAWFORD
LEXINGTON VOLUNTEER FIRE DEPARTMENT	SCOTT
LIVONIA FIRE DEPARTMENT	WASHINGTON
MADISON CITY FIRE DEPARTMENT	JEFFERSON
MADISON TOWNSHIP VOLUNTEER FIRE DEPARTMENT	JEFFERSON
MARENGO - LIBERTY TOWNSHIP FIRE DEPARTMENT	CRAWFORD
MCCULLOCH VOLUNTEER FIRE DEPARTMENT	CLARK
MILLTOWN VOLUNTEER FIRE DEPARTMENT	CRAWFORD
MONROE TOWNSHIP VOLUNTEER FIRE DEPARTMENT	CLARK
NABB VOLUNTEER FIRE DEPARTMENT	CLARK
NEW ALBANY CITY FIRE DEPARTMENT	FLOYD

NEW CHAPEL FIRE COMPANY	FLOYD
NEW MIDDLETOWN VOLUNTEER FIRE DEPARTMENT	HARRISON
NEW WASHINGTON VOLUNTEER FIRE DEPARTMENT	CLARK
ORANGE COUNTY FIREFIGHTERS ASSOCIATION	ORANGE
ORLEANS VOLUNTEER FIRE DEPARTMENT	ORANGE
PALMYRA VOLUNTEER FIRE DEPARTMENT	HARRISON
PAOLI FIRE DEPARTMENT	ORANGE
PEKIN VOLUNTEER FIRE DEPARTMENT	WASHINGTON
PIERCE POLK TOWNSHIP VOLUNTEER FIRE DEPARTMENT	WASHINGTON
POSEY TOWNSHIP VOLUNTEER FIRE DEPARTMENT	WASHINGTON
RAMSEY VOLUNTEER FIRE DEPARTMENT	HARRISON
SALEM VOLUNTEER FIRE DEPARTMENT	WASHINGTON
SCOTTSBURG VOLUNTEER FIRE DEPARTMENT	SCOTT
SELLERSBURG VOLUNTEER FIRE DEPARTMENT	CLARK
SEYMOUR VOLUNTEER FIRE DEPARTMENT	JACKSON
SOUTHEAST VOLUNTEER FIRE DEPARTMENT	ORANGE
SWITZERLAND COUNTY FIRE DEPARTMENTS	SWITZERLAND
UNDERWOOD VOLUNTEER FIRE DEPARTMENTS	CLARK
UTICA TOWNSHIP VOLUNTEER FIRE DEPARTMENT	CLARK
VIENNA TOWNSHIP VOLUNTEER FIRE DEPARTMENT	SCOTT

ACKNOWLEDGEMENTS

There are so many people who make the WHAS Crusade for Children possible we could not list them all. There are literally thousands of people who have been a direct part of the success of the Crusade over the years. While we can't name them all, we want to thank people who have served in various capacities.

Pioneers:

In the research and writing of this book, everyone seems to agree that the courage and vision 50 years ago of Vic Sholis, first General Manager of WHAS and Barry Bingham, Sr., owner of WHAS, Inc. and The Courier-Journal and Louisville Times, made the first Crusade a reality. There has been no stopping it since. Many television and radio professionals over the years lent their expertise and talent to making the Crusade possible

.

Volunteers:

Some of the original volunteers are still with us at this writing. The heart of the Crusade for Children is the corps of volunteers who make the event and the television show possible. They make the sandwiches, answer the phones, drive the golf carts, hold the numbers, hold the cameras, tote the money, count it, guard it and take it to the bank, and everything else in between.

Firefighters:

If the volunteers are the heart, the firefighters are the arms, legs and backs. Starting in 1956, when Chief R.K. Back of the Pleasure Ridge Park Fire Department challenged all fire departments to collect, which is now nearly 200 fire departments from all over Kentucky and Indiana answer the call. The brave men and women of the fire service are what many people think of when they picture the WHAS Crusade for Children. Each year more than 50 per cent of the money raised comes from fire departments. There is a dedicated core of fire department coordinators, currently led by Colonel Joe Bowman from Pleasure Ridge Park, who provide everything from traffic control on Crusade Sunday to muscle throughout the year.

Board Members:

Like any good charity, the WHAS Crusade for Children has an active board of directors. Representatives from WHAS-TV and 84WHAS join fire chiefs, ministers, lawyers, bankers and educators to make sure the Crusade is well managed. Over the years, the pool of talent and expertise has been remarkable.

WHAS-TV Owners and General Managers:

While the WHAS Crusade for Children is a freestanding charity, it takes a television station to make it happen. Everything from free rent to use of the studios and airwaves come from the owners and operators of WHAS-TV. Starting with the Bingham family, passing to the Providence Journal Company and now with Belo, Inc., never in the 50-year history of the Crusade has there been any hesitation by the owners or general managers to support the WHAS Crusade for Children.

Advisory Panel:

The ministers of the "Moral Side of the News" have the difficult job of meeting with each agency that is requesting money from the Crusade. Ministers, priests and rabbis have dedicated hundreds of hours each year to making the tough decisions. Their hard work, dedication, strength and integrity are the heart of the grant process.

Musicians and Entertainers:

The culmination of the annual fund-raising effort is the annual television show. Each year hundreds of entertainers and musicians come together to provide the entertainment. While there is usually a nationally known performer, the local entertainers and musicians are there year after year lending their creative talents and professional skills

.

TV and Radio Employees:

From Belo to Clear Channel to Radio One, employees and their families have been the voices and behind-the-scenes experts making Crusade broadcasts come alive.

Crusade Staff:

A small but dedicated group of people who have the wonderful job of living and working the WHAS Crusade for Children year round.

Thank you also to:

- *Children who sell lemonade and cookies for the Crusade*
- *Employees who pay to dress down on Fridays for the Crusade*
- *Singing cowboys and their sidekicks who loved the Crusade*
- *Every firefighter who ever stood on a road block*
- *Parents who give because they have healthy children*
- *School children who collect their pennies*
- *Employees who give through payroll deduction*
- *Golfers who play in Crusade golf scrambles*
- *Bikers who ride in Crusade "poker runs"*
- *Anglers who fish in Crusade fishing tournaments*
- *Everyone who ever ate a bowl of chili for the Crusade*
- *Everyone who ever bought a chance on an afghan*
- *Little girls who dance in their wheelchairs and prove that miracles do happen*
- *Grown men who cry because they raised more money this year than last*
- *Parents of special needs children who never fail to give*
- *Large corporations that understand how important it is for this community to take care of its own*
- *Small business owners who donate things the Crusade needs*
- *Doctors, nurses, teachers, therapists and educators who take those millions of pennies and do amazing things with them*
- *All the special needs children who are brave, strong and beautiful*

YOU TOO CAN MAKE A DIFFERENCE
IN A CHILD'S LIFE BY DONATING TO THE
WHAS CRUSADE FOR CHILDREN

How can you donate?

You can give annually, put the Crusade in your will or estate planning, purchase a brick in the Walk of Fame, volunteer or donate goods and services to the Crusade.

Annual giving

You can make a monetary contribution to the WHAS Crusade for Children by cash, check, or credit card. Cash or check donations can be made directly through the Crusade office or through your local fire department. All credit card donations can be made online at www.whascrusade.org.

Buy a brick

When you purchase a brick in the WHAS Crusade for Children Walk of Fame, you are making a contribution to the Crusade for Children Endowment. The endowment will cover annual expenses and assure that 100% of every dollar donated continues to directly benefit special needs children.

Estate planning and Memorials

Remember the Crusade during your estate planning. Consider the Crusade in your charitable remainder trust or as the beneficiary of a life insurance plan or 401k program. Many people remember a friend or loved one by making a donation to the WHAS Crusade for Children in memory of the deceased. When you make a memorial contribution, the family of the individual can be notified of your gift.

Volunteer

It takes thousands of volunteers to raise money for the Crusade. There are hundreds of opportunities for you to volunteer with the Crusade year round. Contact your local fire department or the Crusade office to see how you can help.

Donate goods and services

The WHAS Crusade for Children is able to return 100% of all donations to the community because of the generous donations of goods and services from local businesses and individuals. Find out how your company can get involved.

To send a donation or to learn more about the WHAS Crusade for Children contact our offices at:

WHAS Crusade for Children
P.O. Box 1100
Louisville, KY 40201
Phone: (502) 582-7706
Fax: (502) 582-7712
admin@whascrusade.org
www.whascrusade.org

WHAS CRUSADE FOR CHILDREN 27

WHAS CRUSADE FOR CHILDREN 31

The 34th WHAS CRUSADE for CHILDREN

WHAS CRUSADE FOR CHILDREN

WHAS CRUSADE for CHILDREN 35 YEARS OF CARING 1954-1988

17

WHAS Crusade for Children 37

WHAS CRUSADE FOR CHILDREN 36

39th WHAS CRUSADE FOR CHILDREN

CRUSADE WHAS 33 FOR CHILDREN

13

47th WHAS CRUSADE for CHILDREN CRUSADE 2000 1954-2000

WHAS CRUSADE FOR CHILDREN 38

32 CRUSADE FOR CHILDREN WHAS

WHAS CRUSADE FOR CHILDREN 43nd YEAR

WHAS CRUSADE for CHILDREN 50's 60's 70's 80's 90's 46th 1999

WHAS CRUSADE FOR CHILDREN 43 Years 1996

WHAS CRUSADE FOR CHILDREN 41 Years

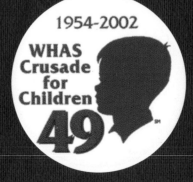
1954-2002 WHAS Crusade for Children 49

WHAS CRUSADE FOR CHILDREN 40 Years